FERTILITY AND HEALTH BEHAVIOUR AMONG HINDU AND MUSLIM WOMEN IN ASSAM

About the Author

Dr. Kishor Singh Rajput, presently a Lecturer in the Department of Economics of St. Anthony's College, Shillong is a triple Master Degree holder in Economics, Population Studies and Ecology and Environment. As a result, his research priorities revolve around themes that allow him to analyse the inter-linkages between population, economic development and environment, mainly at the micro level, so as to have findings that can promote sustainable livelihood in the society.

Fertility and Health Behaviour Among Hindu and Muslim Women in Assam

Kishor Singh Rajput
Lecturer, Deptt. of Economics
St. Anthony's College
Shillong-793001

CONCEPT PUBLISHING COMPANY PVT. LTD.
NEW DELHI-110 059

The publication was financially supported by the ICSSR. The responsibility for the facts stated, opinions expressed or conclusions reached is entirely that of the author and the ICSSR accepts no responsibility for them.

The work was evaluated by Professor A.M. Khan, NIHFW, New Delhi on behalf of the ICSSR.

ISBN-13 : 978-81-8069-780-7

First Published 2011

Published and Printed by

Concept
Since 1974

Concept Publishing Company Pvt. Ltd.
Regd. Office :
A/15-16, Commercial Block, Mohan Garden
New Delhi-110059 (India)
Phones : 25351460, 25351794, *Fax* : 091-11-25357109
Email : publishing@conceptpub.com
Website : www.conceptpub.com

Editorial Office :
H-13, Bali Nagar, New Delhi-110 015, India.

Cataloging in Publication Data--*Courtesy:* D.K. Agencies (P) Ltd. <docinfo@dkagencies.com>

Rajput, Kishor Singh.
Fertility and health behaviour among Hindu and Muslim women in Assam / Kishor Singh Rajput.
p. cm.
Includes bibliographical references (p.) and index.
ISBN 9788180697807

1. Fertility, Human--India-Assam. 2. Reproductive health--India-- Assam. 3. Health behavior--India-- Assam. 4. Hindu women--Health and hygiene--India-- Assam. 5. Muslim women--Health and hygiene--India-- Assam. I. Title.

I dedicate this book

to

my beloved parents

Shri Nanda Singh Rajput

and

Smt. Shanti Devi Rajput

Preface

This book attempts to understand the fertility and health behaviour of women of two different cultural groups, namely Hindus and Muslims. Particular emphasis has been placed on areas such as contraceptive use, son preference, breastfeeding practices, fertility, antenatal care, institutional delivery, etc. among the Hindu and Muslim women and the influence of religion on them. Actually this book examines the reproductive health behaviour of the women in their socio-cultural context to understand the true dynamics of the behaviour from the point of view of religious differentials.

The fertility differential between the Hindus and Muslims is one of the hotly debated topics among the population scientists in India and abroad. Many a times this debate takes political colour and shape that, in turn, influences many political decisions in the country. It is always easy to arouse religious sentiments by picking up few stray figures and drawing conclusions without having any kind of scientific analysis. This book, therefore, studies the differentials in fertility and reproductive health behaviour between the Hindu and Muslim women in a holistic and scientific framework.

This book is a product of the research project, sponsored by the Indian Council of Social Science Research, New Delhi. I put on record my thanks and gratitude to the Council for the financial support.

Dr. C.J. Thomas, Acting Director, ICSSR, North Eastern Regional Centre, Shillong and Dr. Gopal Bardoloi, Selection Grade Lecturer, Handique Girls' College, Guwahati have been a source of inspiration to me. Their guidance and encouragement have immensely helped me at different stages of the project and while writing this book.

My acknowledgement will remain incomplete if I do not mention the significant role played by Dr. Gurudas Dasgupta, Professor, Department of Humanities and Social Sciences, National Institute of Technology, Silchar. It was his advice and encouragement that inspired me to write this book and submit it to the ICSSR, New Delhi for financial support.

My wife, Smt. Meena Devi Rajput, has been a constant source of help and inspiration at all stages of the completion of the project and also in writing this book. I put on record my love and gratitude to my wife for all her efforts so as to free me to focus exclusively on the task in hand. Last but not the least, I would not have been writing this book if I had not had the shower of blessings of my beloved parents—Shri Nanda Singh Rajput and Smt. Shanti Devi Rajput. I am really thankful to both of them for their unconditional love, care and sacrifices made throughout my life.

Kishor Singh Rajput

Contents

List of Tables

List of Figures

1

Introduction

Statement of the Problem

Continuous rapid population growth has remained a major problem in the path of economic development of Assam. For example, Assam's total population increased from 8.02 million in 1951 to 14.62 million in 1971 and further to 26.64 million in 2001—a more than 3 times increase. This magnitude of increase in the population definitely acts as a drag on limited economic resources of the state.

High fertility is an important cause of rapid population growth of Assam. The fertility rates and fertility behaviour vary among the different communities of Assam. Perhaps this is because the various socio-economic variables that determine fertility behaviour of different groups of population affect them differently.

However, the past attempts of the Government to lower the fertility rates of different groups of population failed to a great extent. Most importantly, the fertility reduction policies of the Government in the past failed to take into account the reproductive health needs of the people, particularly that of the married women. High maternal mortality and infant mortality rates, high level of anaemia, etc. are few indicators of the poor situation that exists in the health sector of Assam. However, Government's focus has been reoriented after the International Conference on Population and Development (1994), held in Cairo, as it now puts heavy emphasis on meeting the reproductive health needs of the population in the framework of fertility control programme.

Comprehensive reproductive health programme adopted by consensus at the ICPD, Cairo, in 1994 signifies a paradigm shift in the conventional family planning and population control related approaches. Revolving around women's health as a matter of reproductive right the reoriented health approach aims to address a large number of distinct yet closely interrelated issues which go much beyond conventional family planning and MCH issues. Broadly speaking, client oriented reproductive health programmes try and address issues relating to safe motherhood, abortion, sexually transmitted diseases including HIV/AIDS, family planning, etc.

The Governments all over the World are now trying to incorporate the component of reproductive health in the overall framework of the population policy. The Indian Government as well as the Government of Assam is also now trying its best to meet the reproductive health needs of the people, particularly that of the mother. Keeping in view the paradigm shift in the population policy framework, this book looks into various aspects of fertility and reproductive health behaviour of two major religious communities of Assam, viz., Hindus and Muslims.

Need for the Study

James and Nair (2005) observed that there is ample evidence available in India to suggest a significant variation in fertility across different regions of the country. Even within a state itself, the fertility rate varies across districts. So this present study is the result of the felt need to undertake a detailed study of a district to find out the differences in the fertility and fertility related behaviour of the Hindu and Muslim women.

Furthermore, the past attempts of the Government to lower the fertility levels of different groups of population have, by and large, failed. The past policies were too much targets driven and obsessed with numbers. Consequently, the policies failed to recognize the health aspirations of the people, especially of the married women. But in recent years the focus has shifted towards this aspect of fertility control programme.

As a result, the number of researches undertaken in this area has also increased significantly.

The NFHS-I and NFHS-II surveys have thrown some light on the basic reproductive behaviour of women in Assam, including Hindu and Muslim women. But in the NFHS study, Hindu and Muslim women or religious affiliation has been taken as one of the various socio-economic variables. So a detailed study on the reproductive health behaviour of the Hindu and Muslim women has not been done in Assam, in general and Sonitpur district of Assam, in particular.

Furthermore, as the proposed study will try to explore how the various socio-economic variables like education, occupation, age at marriage, the type of family, family planning practices, etc. affect them (differently or the same way), a greater understanding of the problem in hand is likely to be obtained. The findings, therefore, are likely to throw more light on various aspects of fertility and reproductive health related behaviour of the Hindu and Muslim women. The findings are furthermore likely to be of some help in the future formulation and implementation of a reproductive health delivery system to some extent. We know that if the reproductive health behaviour varies among different groups of population, then the corresponding health delivery system has to approach these groups differently. The present study may help the policy makers to get better insights on the reproductive health behaviour of the Hindu and Muslim women.

Overview of Literature

The fertility rate is very high in Assam as in some other parts of the country (NFHS, Assam, 1992-93). This situation persists basically due to the lower age of marriage, low level of literacy, poor economic status of the couple, large family size, sex consideration/value of children, ignorance, taboos, myths, customs and superstitions and often non-availability of means of reproductive choices (Jain, 1994). In fact, fertility is a very complicated phenomenon and it is affected by social development and cultural change. Fertility is, thus, a multidimensional outcome of all the socio-economic norms and network of couple which are translated through biological reproduction (Mahadevan and Sumangalam, 1987). Furthermore, there are large spatial variations in the religious composition and fertility in India (Alagarajan and Kulkarni, 1998). The striking inter-regional diversity is an important confounding factor in India (Govindasamy and Ramesh, 1997).

Also there exists inter-religion fertility differentials in India. For instance, the mean number of children ever born to Muslims of 3.5 children is significantly higher than Hindus of 2.9 children (Moulasha, 2000). According to the NFHS, 1992-93, the average number of living children for Hindu was 3.0 against the figure of 3.4 for the Muslim. Though the second survey, NFHS-II, 1998-99, showed lower fertility for all the religions, but still the gap between the Hindu and Muslim fertility continued to exist.

Caldwell *et al.* (1988) in his report on "Causes of Fertility Decline in South Asia" maintained that Muslims exhibit significantly higher fertility and are less likely than Hindus to practice family planning. Kulkarni (1996) in his analysis on Hindu and Muslim population growth indicated that the higher growth among Muslims as compared to Hindus was primarily attributable to the higher fertility of Muslims.

On the basis of the analysis of NFHS-II data, Dharmalingam *et al.* (2005) in their article 'Muslim-Hindu Fertility Differences' commented that Muslim-Hindu differences in fertility and contraceptive use are substantial and pervasive across India. A Muslim woman is about 50 per cent more likely to want to have an additional child, and is about half as likely to use contraceptives as a Hindu woman. This result is net of observable socio-economic characteristics at individual, household and district levels, and after taking into account the multi-level structure of data and reality.

Likewise, by analyzing the 2001 Census data on Total Fertility Rate (TFR), Rajan (2005) showed that there was a net difference of TFR of 2.3 between the Muslims and Hindus of Assam as the Muslim TFR was 5.1 and Hindu TFR was 2.8. As far as the Sonitpur district is concerned, the TFR for the Hindus stands at 2.9 as against the TFR of 5.4 for the Muslims. Likewise, other studies (Visaria, 1974; Cassen, 1978; Sharma and Mishra, 1978; Balsubramanian, 1984; Srivastava *et al.*, 1998; Kulkarni, 1996 and Bhat and Zavier, 2005) by using primary as well as secondary data have shown that the Muslims in India exhibit higher level of fertility than the Hindus.

Religion is one of the oldest socio-cultural characteristics associated with the mankind and civilizations created by them over thousands of years of known history. In fact, religion has become a worldwide institution. Its influence is found in all societies and it really acts as a powerful system of social control (Moulasha, 2000). Hence, religion can be considered as an important social attribute. It is of particular importance in our country because we have many faiths and our civilisation is closely linked to religion (Hussain, 1994). India is a country of many religions. Hindus and Muslims are the two major religious communities of India. According to the Census of India, 2001, Hindus constitute 80.46 per cent of the total population of the country, Muslim population's share is 13.43 per cent and the rest is accounted by other religions. However, the religious composition of the population has undergone change over the years. In 1951, for example, the share of the Hindu and Muslim population in the total population stood at 84.9 per cent and 9.9 per cent respectively.

Religion prescribes a code of life, refers to a system of beliefs, attitudes and practices which individuals share in groups, and through this orientation towards life and death, is supposed to affect one's fertility behaviour (Chaudhury, 1982; Ram and Mehta, 1983). This is due to the fact that different communities and people perceive religion in their own unique way (Census of India, 2001).

According to Westoff (1959), religious affiliation of the couple affect the family, directly by imposing sanctions on the practice of the birth control or legitimizing on the practice of less effective methods and indirectly by guiding its members with a moral and social philosophy of marriage and family which emphasize the virtues of reproduction. Clifford (1971) and Jain (1975) observed that belief system and value orientation were important determinants of fertility behaviour and birth control. Religiosity of an individual is a cultural variable and is expected to influence the individual's fertility behaviour (Lorimer, 1954). Borooah and Iyer (2005) in their article 'Religion, Literacy and the Female to Male Ratio' observed that the faster growth rate of the Muslim part of the Indian population is blamed on Indian Muslims' obeying the tenets of Islam in rejecting family planning and embracing polygyny.

Lorimer (1954) considers religiosity of an individual as a cultural variable and, hence, he expects it to influence the individual's fertility behaviour. Kulkarni and Alagarajan (2005) in their article "Population Growth, Fertility and Religion in India" opined that higher than average fertility among Muslims is on account of the religion factor, be it theological or of minority position. Furthermore, they have found strong effect of religion on the contraceptive use of the Muslims. However, Borooah and Iyer (2005) suggested that there is no consensus in India as to how much influence Islam has on contraception and marriage and ultimately on fertility.

However, the seed of the debate on the differential population growth rates of the Hindus and Muslims was planted in the undivided India itself. Kingsley Davis, an eminent demographer, was one of the first to raise a debate on the Hindu-Muslim population growth rates in the sub-continent. In his famous book "The Population of India and Pakistan" (1951), he presented before the world the fact that Muslim fertility was higher than the Hindu fertility. For instance, the decline in the proportion of the Hindus from 75.1 per cent to 72.9 per cent in between the censuses of 1881 and 1901 (Davis, 1951) created strong reaction and fear among the Hindus that the Muslims would become the majority population in India in the future.

Numerous research and review studies have been done on this area since then. But there seems to be no end to this highly debated topic and it still remains a very popular area for research studies among the research scholars and population scientists.

Basu (1997) refers to this whole debate as nothing but the politicization of fertility whereby criticisms are levelled against the Muslims on demographic front for non-demographic interventions in Muslim lives. But Ashish Bose (1969) in his article "Differential Fertility by Religion in India" terms this problem as a technical problem rather than a political problem in demographic analysis. It is always easy to quote stray figures and mislead the people and arouse passions. He, therefore, urges the demographers and statisticians to analyse this problem in a scientific manner and place before the country the findings of their studies. In other words, it is important to go beyond the population growth rate figures of Hindus and Muslims and give a thought to other demographic, economic and social variables (Bose, 2005).

Many other scholars, however, object using religion as an explanatory variable in understanding demographic change (Ludden, 1996; Jeffrey and Jeffrey, 1997; Jeffrey and Jeffrey, 2002). According to them, in addition to directly influencing fertility through the proximate determinants, religion can also impact fertility indirectly through socio-economic factors. Religion can differentially affect or be related to the distribution of individual and group characteristics which then influence reproductive behaviour.

They also conclude that Muslims are less educated and are in weaker economic positions than Hindus. Schooling and some other socio-economic aspects have very strong bearing on fertility—much stronger than the relationship with religion. The socio-economic factors, therefore, have important bearing on fertility (Rajendran, 1997; Manna, 1998). Since socio-economic variables are known to be associated with fertility, the religious differentials in these can plausibly cause differentials in fertility (Shariff, 1994, 1995 and Jeffrey and Jeffrey, 1997). For Moulasha (2000) also, the determinants of Hindu fertility were different from that of Muslim fertility. He has found out that the variables that were influencing the fertility of Hindus and Muslims were not the same.

Jeffrey and Jeffrey (2000 and 2002) observed that Muslims are not a homogeneous group in respect of their socio-economic and demographic behaviour in different regions of the country. For instance, the Muslims are found closer to Hindus in respect of their socio-economic and demographic behaviour in a particular region of the country than they do with the Muslims living elsewhere in the country. Thus, Bhagat and Praharaj (2005) observed that the fertility levels and differentials among Muslims within India, as well as across Muslim countries, indicate that reproductive behaviour among Muslims is essentially not uniform; there are factors other than religion, which are even more important. Therefore, they commented that the relatively higher fertility among the Muslims cannot be understood independent of its socio-economic and political contexts.

Consequently one of the important hypotheses for the religious differentials of fertility suggested by many research scholars (Jones and Nortman, 1968; Kirk, 1968, Goldscheider and Uhlenberg, 1969 and Chamie, 1977) is that of characteristics, i.e. the socio-economic characteristics could vary by religion causing fertility differentials. However, it is also true that considerable disagreement exists among the population scientists as to how far socio-economic disparities can explain the fertility differential (Bhat and Zavier, 2005). As such it can be said that population of different religions that vary in factors such as education, income, occupation, etc. could actually lead to differential fertility. The religious differential in fertility can, therefore, be considered as the product of the differences in the socio-economic characteristics and the influence of these characteristics on fertility.

The results of the MCA analyses of the NFHS-II data for the major states of India by Kulkarni and Alagarajan (2005) countered the characteristic hypothesis. Moulasha (2000) also arrived at the same conclusion. In other words, socio-economic factors do not seem to explain the religious differentials in fertility. However, literatures also exist to show that Hindu-Muslim differences in observed fertility might not be real (Dharmalingam and Morgan, 2004). As a result, Hindu-Muslim fertility differentials disappear once the background socio-economic variables are controlled.

For Kulkarni and Alagarajan (2005), religious as well as other differences in fertility are inevitable during fertility transition—the process of decline from high fertility in the past to voluntarily regulated low fertility. This happens because sections, whether regions or religions, do not transit from a high fertility regime to a low fertility regime at the same time or pace. Therefore, at a given point of time, those ahead in this process would have lower fertility than those lagging—thus opening a wide gap. India is currently undergoing the process of fertility transition and there is irrefutable evidence that fertility has declined substantially in all the major religious communities in India over the period of time.

Contrary to fertility studies, research on women's reproductive health and reproductive rights is considered as a neglected area (Lane, 1994; McDaniel, 1996, 2000; and Freedman 1999). A distinctive gender-related and health-related aspect of much demographic research today is on the assumption that women are the keepers of a nation's health (Basu, 2000). The role of women as primary custodians of family health should be recognised and supported (United Nations, 1995).

Therefore, it is very necessary that studies and research activities are undertaken on issues like men and women's perceptions and current health seeking behaviour in different settings of population, viz., urban, rural, slum, etc. and on various health aspects like antenatal care, pregnancy complications, child survival, immunisation of the mother and child and so on (GoI, 1997). However, the knowledge that exists in this field can be considered as the tip of iceberg only.

Maternal health requires urgent attention, as there is an extraordinary difference in maternal death rates between the developed and developing countries (ICMR, 1990). According to the World Bank (1993), about one-third of the total disease burden of women of 15 to 44 years of age in developing countries is linked to health problems related to pregnancy. Every minute of everyday a woman dies as a result of pregnancy or childbirth. Every time a woman in the Third World becomes pregnant, her risk of dying is 200 times higher than the risk run by a woman in the developed World (Motashaw, 1997). In many developing countries about 50 per cent of pregnancy terminations occur among the high-risk mothers (Rinchart and Kols, 1984).

In developing countries older women usually have many children and women who marry young may have several closely spaced births before they reach the age of 20. Among these pregnancies, there are greater risks of miscarriage, stillbirths and deaths during infancy (Swenson and Harpner, 1979; Chen *et al.*, 1974; Koenig *et al.*, 1988). Pregnancies of younger mothers (below 18 years) and older mothers (over 35 years), too many pregnancies (5 or more) and closer birth interval of less than 24 months are likely to produce high risks to mothers and child life (Perkin, 1968).

Chatterjee (1996) stresses that women in India bear their health problems in a 'culture of silence' and do not seek timely health care; they often cannot travel beyond the area of their normal activities to obtain services; they cannot usually approach male health providers; in general, families, including women themselves, spend less time, effort and money seeking health care for women and girls than men. There are substantial data to show that Indian women also bear a heavy burden of reproductive morbidity (Bang and Bang, 1991 and Pachauri, 1994). The fact that 1,00,000 women in India are estimated to die every year from pregnancy and child-birth related causes reinforces the importance of ensuring that all pregnant women receive adequate antenatal care during pregnancy and the deliveries take place under the supervision of trained medical personnel in a hygienic environment (IIPS, 1995).

Traditionally, women in India have been associated with home while the men with the world of work. This compartmentalization has led to gender differentiation of an order that distinguishes men and women. As a result, the females in the society are being led by the cultural traditions and religious beliefs rather than legal rights (Ashraf, 1994). Therefore, the need to emphasize reproductive health as a matter of human right issue cannot be exaggerated (Rajput, 2002).

Only in 1995, the Ministry of Health and Family Welfare introduced the Reproductive and Child Health Programme (RCH) as a part of 'Paradigm Shift' in its ongoing family welfare programme (Kumar, 2002). All these changes have followed the International Conference on Population and Development (ICPD), held in Cairo, in 1994. The Programme of Action formulated at the end of the Cairo Conference postulated that population policies should be viewed as an integral part of programmes for women's development, women's rights, women's reproductive health, poverty alleviation and sustainable development. In recent years, particularly after the Cairo Conference (1994), researchers from all over the World have started putting more and more emphasis on various reproductive health issues, specially that of married women.

Like fertility, reproductive health behaviour of different religious groups may vary considerably. Recently, interest has grown in examining community influences on individual health outcomes, so as to place health-care seeking behaviour in its socio-economic context (Manda, 1998; Magadi *et al.*, 2000; and Chacko, 2001). Studies have shown that the use of reproductive health care services is influenced by individual and household characteristics. Studies of health service use highlight a range of modifying factors in a woman's propensity to seek health care that include demographic, socio-economic and health experience characteristics (Becker *et al.*, 1977 and Stephenson and Tsui, 2002). Khan (1990) also maintains that knowledge and utilisation of reproductive health care services in different communities in India is intimately associated with traditional beliefs, customs and the individual's background characteristics. The different socio-economic and cultural practices ultimately have a bearing on maternal and child health and family welfare services.

Various socio-economic and demographic factors that have been considered as having important bearing on health problems and the likelihood of health service use are urban residence (Addai, 1998), household living conditions (Bloom *et al.*, 1999; Magadi *et al.*, 2000), household income (Kavitha and Audinarayana, 1997), occupational status (Nwakoby, 1994; Miles-Doan and Brewster, 1998; Nuwaha and Amooti-kaguna,

1999), the type of family in which they live and their status (Ashraf, 1994), woman's employment in skilled work outside the home (Addai, 1998; Miles-Doan and Brewster, 1998; Estrin, 1999), husband's high level of education (Nwakoby, 1994; Nuwaha and Amooti-kaguna, 1999), low parity (Bhatia and Cleland, 1995a; Kavitha and Audinarayana, 1997; Magadi *et al.*, 2000) and young maternal age (Bhatia and Cleland, 1995a). Hobcraft (1993) and Desai (1994) have also established the linkage between mother's schooling and her reproductive health behaviour. Educated women are better able to break away from tradition to utilize modern health care services for safeguarding their own health and that of their children (Caldwell and Caldwell, 1988; Cleland, 1990). Educated women are better able to utilize what is available in the community to their advantage (Barrera, 1990; Caldwell, 1990; Goodburn *et al.*, 1990) and may be able to make independent decisions regarding their own and their children's health leading to greater utilization of modern health facilities (Caldwell, 1979; Caldwell, 1986).

Kapadia (1999) also believes that high levels of mortality and morbidity of the women are affected by a complex interplay of biological, economic, socio-cultural and psychological factors throughout their lives. So, there is the need to consider women's health problems in the context of their empowerment.

However, the various socio-economic and demographic factors are quite often mediated by cultural influences that shape the way an individual perceives his or her own health and the health services available (Basu, 1990; Obermeyer, 1993; Bhatia and Cleland, 1995b; Goodburn *et al.*, 1995).

Community beliefs and norms relating to health care seeking behaviours are reflected in individuals' decisions, which are based, to some degree, on how they think the community views their actions (Rutenberg and Watkins, 1997). Community beliefs concerning childbearing preferences and sexual and reproductive health behaviour exert a strong influence on individual attitudes towards family planning and fertility preferences (Greenwell, 1996). Similarly, traditional beliefs surrounding childbirth coupled with misconceptions about and fear of medical institutions act to maintain women's reliance on home delivery in India (Basu, 2000; Griffiths and Stephenson, 2001). Therefore, it can be said that though socio-economic factors are key determinants of health behaviour and the service use, the individual's cultural environment influences the extent to which these factors can lead to service use.

Recently, that is why, interest has grown among research scholars in examining community influences on individual health outcomes, so as to place health care seeking behaviour in its socio-economic context (Entwisle and Mason 1985; Entwisle *et al.*, 1989; Von Korff *et al.*,1992; Pebley *et al.*, 1996; DeGraff *et al.*, 1997; Manda, 1998; Magadi *et al.* 2000; and Chacko, 2001). These studies relate individual health outcomes and health care seeking behaviour to the socio-economic characteristics of the community.

Objectives of the Study

The proposed project mainly aims to explore certain important areas of fertility and basic reproductive health behaviour of Hindu and Muslim women. The specific objectives of the proposed study are:

1. to find out the existing level of fertility and fertility behaviour among Hindus and Muslims.
2. to find out the effect of important socio-economic variables of fertility and fertility behaviour among Hindus and Muslims.
3. to find out the maternal health care experience of these communities of Assam, viz., the maternal health problems, treatment behaviour and avenues of treatment seeking, in case of health problems.
4. to find out the effect of important socio-economic variables on the basic reproductive health behaviour of Hindus and Muslims.

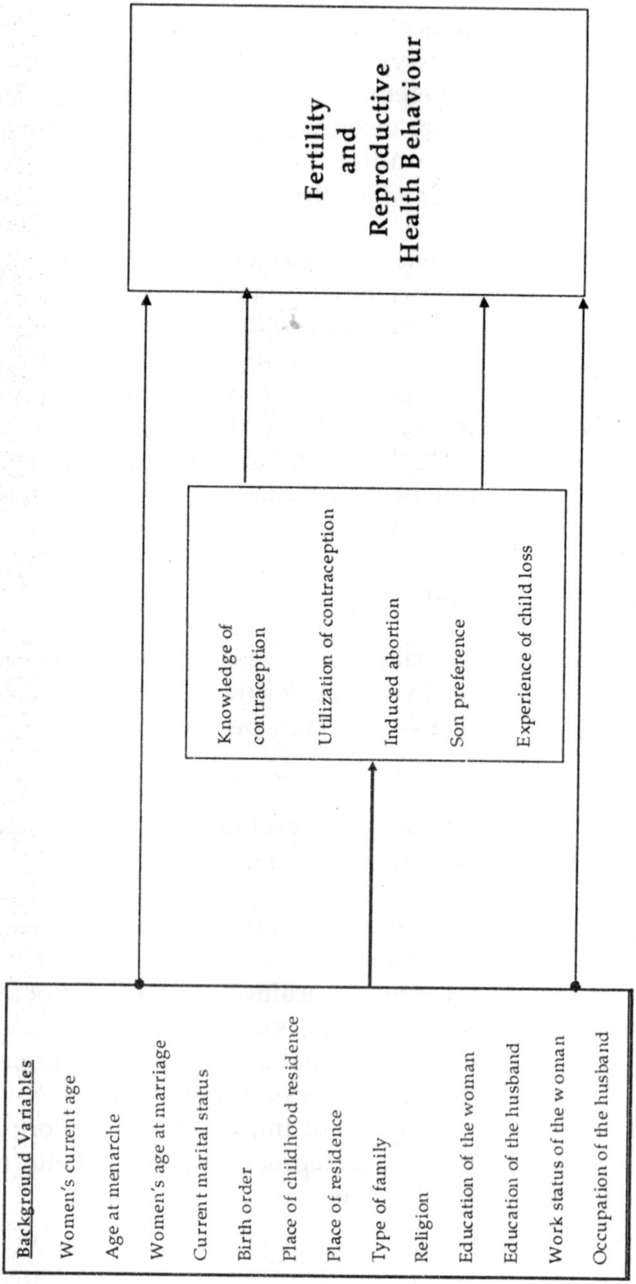

Fig. 1.1 : Conceptual framework used for the study

2

Research Methodology

Sample Design

The sample design adopted for the study is that of a multistage technique, fitted to the requirements of the study.

There are three subdivisions in the Sonitpur district of Assam, namely Tezpur, Biswanath and Gohpur subdivisions. For the rural sample, in the first stage, one block each from the above three subdivisions were selected. The blocks so chosen were the Gabharu Development Block from the Tezpur Subdivision, Baghmora Development Block from the Biswanath Subdivison and Chaiduar Development Block from the Gohpur Subdivision. In the next stage, two Gaon Panchayats (G.Ps.) from each block were selected and then three villages were selected purposefully to meet the requirements of the study. The villages were chosen in such a manner so as to have Hindu and Muslim population with similar socio-economic set up to the extent possible. The villages so chosen are—

Darikial Gaon (Ushapur G.P.), Barika Chuburi Muslim Gaon (Ushapur G.P.) and Kariyani Bangali (Rajgarh G.P.) in the Gabharu Development Block of Tezpur Subdivision.

Niz Baghmari (Niz Baghmari G.P.) and Mauza Basti (Borjaroni G.P.) in the Baghmora Development Block of Biswanath Subdivision.

Aribhanga (Missamari G.P.), Amlokhi Doloni (Missamari G.P.), Missamari (Missamari G.P.) and Nalanibari (Nalanibari G.P.) in the Chaiduar Development Block of Gohpur Subdivison.

Table 2.1: Distribution of the Total Sample—Block-wise and Town-wise

Area	*Hindu*	*Muslim*
Gabharu Development Block	**35 (14.3)**	**54 (20.9)**
Darikial Gaon	35	—
Kariyani Bangali	—	22
Barika Chuburi Muslim Gaon	—	32
Baghmora Development Block	**35 (14.3)**	**41 (15.9)**
Mauza Basti	—	10
Niz Baghmari	35	31
Chaiduar Development Block	**52 (21.2)**	**46 (17.8)**
Aribhanga	22	—
Nalanibari	—	30
Amlokhi Doloni	19	16
Missamari	11	—
Tezpur Town	**39 (15.9)**	**35 (13.6)**
Biswanath Chariali Town	**42 (17.1)**	**41 (15.9)**
Gohpur Town	**42 (17.1)**	**41 (15.9)**
Total	**245 (100.0)**	**258 (100.0)**

* Figures in the parentheses are in percentage

As far as the urban population is concerned, Tezpur town from the Tezpur Subdivision and Biswanath Chariali town from the Biswanath Subdivision were selected randomly. In the Gohpur Subdivision, there was only one urban centre, viz. Gohpur town and, hence, it was selected for the study. After the selection of the towns, the wards in the above-mentioned towns having both Hindu and Muslim population were identified and selected for the purpose of the study.

In the next stage, lists of all households having the eligible women were prepared for each village and ward. In the last stage, using the simple random sampling technique, data were collected from a total of 503 women with 245 being the Hindu women and the remaining 258 being the Muslim women. Table 2.1 provides a detailed picture of the entire sample population—village-wise and town-wise.

Data Collection: Tools and Techniques

For the purpose of collection of data, a pre-coded structured interview schedule was prepared and then required data were collected from the women by direct interview method. The interview schedule had four sections. Section I contained questions that were aimed at measuring the standard of living of the woman's family. Section II contained questions relating to the background socio-economic characteristics of the respondent and her family; Questions concerning women's fertility and related behaviour like knowledge and use of contraception, desire for additional children, etc. were included in Section III; In Section IV, questions were asked about the utilization of the antenatal care facilities, services received during antenatal care, types of problems during antenatal, natal and post-natal period and avenues treatment seeking in case of health problems. **(Appendix A).**

Since the respondents were women and the questions were related to their reproductive health behaviour, it was decided to have a well-qualified team of two female field investigators and a research officer. A ten days long training programme was organized for the investigators and the research officer wherein the interview schedule was explained to them in detail. They were also trained so as to collect the requisite data from the sample women as accurate and reliable as possible.

Once they became well acquainted with the questions, they were sent to the field on trial basis for data collection, along with the research supervisor. Afterwards, the various problems encountered in the field were discussed threadbare and ways and means were worked out to handle those situations. Though most of the times, the research officer accompanied the investigator to the household, but the privacy was always maintained to the extent possible between the investigator and the respondent at the time of interview.

Before going to the field, the interview schedule was pre-tested. The pre-testing helped to find out few minor anomalies that existed in the interview schedule. Consequently, needed changes were effected in the original interview schedule for the collection of the required data. Furthermore, the interview was mainly conducted in Assamese language to get more accurate and reliable answer. The team of the investigators was specifically trained for this and they were also given a copy of the interview schedule translated into Assamese language. Utmost care was taken not to distort the meaning of various questions and the coded answers when they were translated into Assamese language. Conscious efforts were always made to check each interview schedule before leaving the village about their completion. If any error or mistake was detected, then the respondent was again re-visited to rectify the mistake. The actual survey was conducted during the period of April 2006 tc July 2006. On an average, one interview lasted for about 60 minutes.

Field Experiences

Before the collection of the data from the field, efforts were made to develop good rapport with the headmen, distinguished persons, social workers, health workers, etc. of the selected rural areas. Many of them came forward quite willingly and whole-heartedly to help to carry out the interviews in their villages. However, negative remarks and non-co-operation were also encountered from certain quarters during the data collection period. Particularly some quarters of the Muslim society were quite skeptical about the whole exercise.

As far as the respondents were concerned, many of them came forward willingly for the interview and their husbands and in-laws also helped to carry out the interviews. However, some of the respondents tried to shy away from the investigators, but came forward for the interviews only after long persuasion and encouragements. Likewise, some other respondents and their family members enquired about the monetary benefits that they would get from the entire exercise. Once the reason behind the study was explained to them, some got satisfied, whereas some others still insisted to remember them in case of implementation of any benefit programme in future. Even in one or two villages, few women who were not selected for the survey insisted on giving the interviews, thinking that they would derive some benefits in future from the whole exercise.

Since most of the questions were related to the health, few women even tried to seek medical advice from the investigators on their health problems, thinking that they were health professionals. In some cases, the investigators had to wait for a long time to meet the selected respondents to complete the interviews. Furthermore, in the Muslim dominated villages, some of the families did not allow the respondents to give the interview, arguing that the data might be used for other than research purpose. Only after explaining properly the purpose and objective behind the study and after showing the letter containing declaration that the data shall only be used for research purpose and signed by the Project Director, they came forward for the interview.

In the urban areas also, with few exceptions, the investigators did not face much hardship in the collection of data. However, the investigators had to adjust their time and make re-visit to some households to meet the working women. In the urban areas, some people enquired about the financial support derived for the study. They wanted to know whether the study was a part of any project funded by any N.G.O. or Government agency and, hence, the financial benefits derived from the project. The research officer and the investigators always tried to meet the queries of these people to their satisfaction.

Data Analysis and Interpretation

After the collection of data from the field, for some of the un-coded information contained in the interview schedule, coding was done and then they were entered in the computer using the SPSS 10.0 for Windows.

In order to arrive at meaningful conclusions, appropriate statistical techniques have been used. To begin with, bivariate analysis has been used to study Hindu-Muslim differentials in the age at marriage, use of contraception, mean number of children ever born, antenatal care, breastfeeding practice, awareness on STDs, etc. In order to determine the effect of religious differential of the women on dependent variables, such as fertility, use of contraception, utilization of antenatal care services, place of delivery, etc., statistical techniques, namely, multiple classification analysis and logistic regression have been used. These techniques have been basically used in the present study to determine the effect of religious differential of the women on the dependent variables by controlling the effect of the other selected background/predictor variables. A brief theoretical background of the above-mentioned statistical techniques used in the study have been presented in the **Appendix B.**

3

Profile of the Study Area and the Respondents

Profile of the Study Area

The study area of the present project is Sonitpur district of Assam.

Assam

The origin of the name Assam is derived from the Sanskrit word *'Asom'*, meaning unparalleled. The ancient Assam was known as *Pragjyotisha* in the Mahabharata and *Kamrupa* in the Puranas and Tantras.

Physically, the present boundary of the state is lying between 24° to 28° north latitudes and 84°40′to 96° east longitudes. It is bounded in the north by the neighbouring country of Bhutan and the Indian state of Arunachal Pradesh; in the east by the states of Arunachal Pradesh, Nagaland and Manipur; in the south by Bangladesh and the states of Mizoram, Tripura and Meghalaya; and in the west by Bangladesh and the state of West Bengal. Assam has two distinct physical divisions, namely the Brahmaputra Valley and the Barak Valley.

Geographically, the present Assam is a shadow of her former self. In 1948, the North East Frontier Agency (NEFA) was separated from Assam. In 1957, Nagaland was carved out of Assam as a Centrally Administered Area and was accorded the statehood in 1961. Then Meghalaya was created as an autonomous state in 1970 and became a full-fledged state in

1972. In the same year, Mizoram came into being as a Union Territory and was conferred the statehood in 1987.

Economically, Assam is predominantly an agriculture-based economy. The principal food crop is rice, though cash crops like tea, sugarcane, oil seeds, etc. are also grown in the state. The industrial sector of the economy is, however, not well developed, though the state is well-endowed with natural resources like crude oil, natural gas, coal, limestone, etc.

Culturally, the state of Assam is inhabited by many general caste, scheduled caste and scheduled tribe population. The main tribes of Assam are Bodos, Kacharis, Mishings, Rabhas, Karbis, Deuris, Tiwas, Dimasas, Chutias, Hmars and Lalungs. Bihu is the major cultural festival of Assam. Assamese is the official language of the state. However, Bengali is recognized as the official language in the Bengali speaking Barak Valley districts of Cachar, Karimganj and Hailakandi.

Demographically, Assam is the most populous state in the North East India with a total population of 2.67 crores (Census of India, 2001). Over the years, Assam's population has grown quite rapidly. Along with this rapid population growth, there has taken place distinctive changes in the religious composition of the population of the state (Rajput, 2001). For example, according to the Census of India figures, the Hindu population increased from 66.65 per cent in 1951 to 72.51 per cent in 1971, mainly due to the separation of the Christian population dominated states from Assam. However, the share of the Hindu population in total population again declined to 64.89 per cent in 2001. On the other hand, the Muslim population in Assam continuously increased from 22.60 per cent in 1951 to 24.56 per cent in 1971 and further to 30.92 per cent in 2001. Assam accounts for 6.0 per cent of the total Muslim population in India. According to the 2001 Census, Assam ranks second among all states of India in terms of percentage of Muslim population to total population.

Sonitpur District

The Sonitpur district of Assam came into being when the Darrang district was segregated into two independent districts, namely Darrang district and Sonitpur district. Sonitpur district is located in the Brahmaputra Valley of Assam. The district is surrounded by North Lakhimpur district on the east, Darrang district on the west, Arunachal Pradesh on the north and the mighty river Brahmaputra on the south.

Sonitpur district is inhabited people of different religions and ethnicity. Hindus and Muslims are the two main religious communities of Assam. According to the Census of India, 2001, the total population of the district stood at 16.82 lakhs with Hindu and Muslim population accounting for 76.58 per cent and 15.94 per cent of the total population respectively. Christianity is mainly embraced by the some sections of the tribal population as well as the tea garden communities of Assam and their share in the total population stands at 6.88 per cent. Rest of the population is accounted by other religions.

Ethnicity-wise, besides the general population, the district of Sonitpur is mainly inhabited by tribes like Mishings, Bodos, Kacharis, etc. Due to the existence of many tea gardens in the district, the tea garden communities hold a significant place in the ethnic composition of the population of the district. These tea garden tribes mainly migrated from states like Jharkhand, Chhattisgarh, Orissa, etc. during the British period and since then have permanently settled in Assam.

Profile of the Respondents

This section (Table 3.1) highlights the background characteristics of the respondents and the family.

Current age of the women

On the basis of three stages of women's reproductive life, the age of the women has been divided into three categories, namely 15-24, 25-34 and 35-49 for the present study.

Maximum number of women for both Hindu and Muslim belong to the age group 25-34. Around 55.0 per cent of the sample Hindu women and around 51 per cent of the Muslim women belong to this group. The percentage of Hindu and Muslim women in the age group 15-24 is 15.1 per cent and

Table 3.1: Per cent distribution of Hindu and Muslim women according to their background characteristics

Background characteristics	Hindu	Muslim
Current age of the women		
15-24	15.1 (37)	22.1 (57)
25-34	55.1 (135)	50.8 (131)
35-49	29.8 (73)	27.1 (70)
Age at menarche		
Below 10 years	7.3 (18)	9.3 (24)
Between 10-14 years	87.3 (214)	86.0 (222)
After 14 years	5.3 (13)	4.7 (12)
Age at marriage of the women		
Before 18 years	20.4 (50)	50.0 (129)
After 18 years	79.6 (195)	50.0 (129)
Marital status of the women		
Currently married	95.9 (235)	94.2 (243)
Separated/Divorced	0.4 (1)	1.9 (5)
Widowed	3.7 (9)	3.9 (10)
Place of childhood residence		
Rural	65.7 (161)	66.3 (171)
Urban	34.3 (84)	33.7 (87)
Current place of residence		
Rural	49.8 (122)	54.7 (141)
Urban	50.2 (123)	45.3 (117)
Type of the family		
Nuclear	65.3 (160)	74.0 (191)
Joint	34.7 (85)	26.0 (67)
Education of the women		
Illiterate	11.4 (28)	37.6 (97)
Less than middle school	35.5 (87)	43.4 (112)
Middle school and above	53.1 (130)	19.0 (49)
Work status of the women		
Not working	86.9 (213)	93.4 (241)
Working	13.1 (32)	6.6 (17)
Husband's education		
Illiterate	8.1 (19)	32.7 (81)
Less than middle school	31.4 (74)	42.7 (106)
Middle school and above	60.6 (143)	24.6 (61)
Occupation of the husband		
Agriculturists/farmers	16.5 (39)	6.9 (17)
Service holders	35.6 (84)	9.3 (23)
Businessmen	33.9 (80)	57.3 (142)
Others	14.0 (33)	26.6 (66)
Standard of living of the family		
Low	43.3 (106)	62.0 (160)
High	56.7 (139)	38.0 (98)
Media exposure of the women		
Low	22.0 (54)	45.3 (117)
Medium	59.6 (146)	48.1 (124)
High	18.4 (45)	6.6 (17)

22.1 per cent respectively. In the highest age group of 35-49, the percentage share of Hindu and Muslim women were 29.8 per cent and 27.1 per cent respectively.

Age at menarche

As far as the age at menarche of the respondents is concerned, 87.3 per cent of the Hindu women and 86.0 per cent of the Muslim women had their puberty between the ages 10 to 14 years.

Age at marriage of the women

The legal age at marriage for girl in India is 18 years. But the data show that many of the respondents got married before they attained the legal age of marriage. For example, half of the Muslim respondents said that they had got married before the age of 18 years. However, only 20.4 per cent of the Hindu women reported to have married before the attainment of legal age at marriage.

Marital status of the women

The marital status of 95.9 per cent of the Hindu respondents and 94.2 per cent of the Muslim respondents were currently married. 3.7 per cent of the Hindu women and 3.9 per cent of the Muslim women were widowed, whereas the percentages of separated/divorced Hindu and Muslim women were 0.4 per cent and 1.9 per cent respectively.

Place of childhood residence

The place of childhood residence can have great impact on a person's life. When the sample data are cross-classified according to the place of childhood residence, it is seen that 65.7 of the Hindu women and 66.3 per cent of the Muslim women lived in the rural areas during their childhood.

Current place of residence

As far as the current place of residence is concerned, half of the sampled Hindu women live in the rural area and the remaining half in the urban area, whereas 54.7 per cent of the Muslim women belong to the rural area and the remaining 45.3 per cent belongs to the urban area.

Type of the family

The type of family in which a woman lives may also affect her fertility behaviour. For instance, a woman living in a nuclear family may have more freedom to exercise her own decisions and choices, which may not be possible for a woman living in a joint family.

The data portray that majority of the Hindu and Muslim women live in the nuclear family. Nearly two-third of the Hindu women (i.e. 65.3 per cent) live in the nuclear family, whereas three-fourth of the Muslim women (i.e. 74 per cent) live in the nuclear family.

Education level of the women

In the field of education, we can see a striking difference between the Hindu and Muslim women. The percentage of illiterate Hindu women is 11.4 per cent whereas the respective figure for the Muslim women is 37.6 per cent. But for the highest educational category of middle school and above as used in the study, the percentage of Hindu women stands at 53.1 per cent, whereas only 19.0 per cent of the Muslim women belongs to this category. The percentages of the Hindu and Muslim women having less than middle school education stands 35.5 and 43.4 respectively.

Work status of the women

In traditional Indian society, household is the domain of work for most of the women. A woman is generally not expected to go out of house for work and earn livelihood for the family. But working women, because of their financial independence and higher educational qualification in all probability, can take certain important decisions that are in the best interests of herself, her children and the family—if necessary even by breaking the age-old traditional myths and taboos.

In conformity with the feature of a traditional society, majority of the Hindu and Muslim women have been found to be engaged in household activities. Only 13.1 per cent and 6.6 per cent of Hindu and Muslim women respectively have been found out to be working outside their home.

Education level of the husband

As it can be seen from Table 3.1, the lowest percentage (8.1 per cent) of the Hindu husbands falls in the illiterate category and the highest percentage (60.6 per cent) in the category of middle school and above. On the contrary, the highest percentage (42.7 per cent) of the Muslim husbands fall in the educational category of less than middle school and the lowest (24.6 per cent) in the category of middle school passed and above. In other words, the husbands of the Hindu women have been found to be more educationally advanced than the husbands of the Muslim women.

Occupation of the husband

The distribution of the respondents' husbands according to their occupation also shows marked variation. For example, 16.5 per cent of the husbands of the Hindu women are engaged in the traditional activity of agriculture/farming compared to 6.9 per cent of the husbands of the Muslim women. As far as the occupation of service is concerned, majority of the Hindu husbands (35.6 per cent) are engaged in it, whereas for the Muslim husbands, the corresponding figure is 9.3 per cent. In the occupation of business, more Muslim husbands are engaged (57.3 per cent) than the Hindus (33.9 per cent).

Standard of living of the family

Many population scientists term development as the best contraceptive. Hence, the standard of living of the family can be considered as an important variable affecting fertility behaviour. The standard of living index (**Appendix C**) constructed on the basis of the data collected on the economic conditions of the family has been divided into two categories, namely low standard of living and high standard of living.

When the women are categorized by the standard of living of the family, it is seen 56.7 per cent of the Hindu women belong to the high group in comparison to 38.0 per cent of the Muslim women. On the other hand, against 43.3 per cent of the Hindu women belonging to low group, 62.0 per cent of the Muslim women come from the low group.

Media exposure of the women

The exposure to mass media is an important factor that can engineer positive attitudinal changes in a society. The level of media exposure of the women determined on the basis of women's exposure to newspaper, T.V. and radio shows that 22.0 per cent of the Hindu women and 45.3 per cent of the Muslim women can be considered as having low exposure. Compared to 18.4 of the Hindu women, only 6.6 per cent of the Muslim women have been found to have high media exposure.

4

Fertility and Its Related Behaviour

Bongaarts in 1978 came out with a synthetic framework of fertility with eight proximate determinants, namely, proportion of women married, use of contraception, induced abortion, lactational infecundability, frequency of intercourse, sterility, spontaneous intra-uterine mortality and duration of fertile period. The purified version of the framework of fertility consists of only four proximate determinants fertility, viz., proportion of women married, use of contraception, induced abortion and postpartum amenorrhoea (Bongaarts and Potter, 1983). So this section tries to throw light about the fertility related behaviour of the Hindu and Muslim women in areas like contraception, breastfeeding, son preference, abortion, etc.

Contraception

Greater contraceptive use is the key mechanism through which accelerated fertility reduction strategies are adopted in India (James and Nair, 2005). Correct knowledge and information of various modern contraceptives may help in the accelerated use of these methods. However, that may again depend on certain other factors. For example, social institutions, cultural and religious constraints, patriarchy, marriage by choice, economic security and social protection provided by family, son preference, etc. are some factors that affect the use of contraceptives (Roy *et al.* 1997). Likewise, infant and child mortality may exert negative effect on contraceptive use (Rahman, 1996).

The difference in the contraceptive use is frequently cited as the prime factor contributing to religious differentials in fertility. It has often been said that Islam bars its followers from using contraceptives, though there is no absolute consensus on the matter (Khan, 1979; Omran, 1992). Therefore, in order to have a better understanding of religious differentials in fertility, one must examine the differentials in contraceptive use (Kulkarni and Alagarajan, 2005). This section provides information about the women's knowledge of various family planning methods, their current use and also reasons of non-use.

Knowledge and use of contraception by methods

Data presented in Table 4.1 indicate the level of knowledge and use of various contraceptives of the ever-married women as obtained by spontaneous responses. The knowledge of the family planning methods is found quite widespread amongst both Hindu and Muslim women. Around 98 per cent of the Hindu women and approximately 93 per cent of the Muslim women know about the contraceptives.

As far as specific methods are concerned, 76.3 per cent and 69.0 per cent of the Hindu and Muslim women respectively are found to know about the female sterilization. On the other hand, the knowledge of male sterilisation is found among 65.3 per cent and 54.3 per cent of Hindu and Muslim women respectively.

The knowledge of spacing methods like oral pills and condom is indeed found very good amongst the Hindu and Muslim women. The knowledge of copper-T, oral pills and condom is found among 80.0 per cent, 85.3 per cent and 93.1 per cent of the Hindu women respectively. The respective percentages for the Muslim women are 56.2 per cent, 77.9 per cent and 80.6 per cent respectively.

Regarding the traditional methods of periodic abstinence and withdrawal, 58.4 per cent and 48.2 per cent of the Hindu women have been found to have the knowledge. The percentages of the Muslim women knowing about periodic abstinence and withdrawal method are 43.0 per cent and 31.8 per cent respectively.

Table 4.1: Per cent distribution of the Hindu and Muslim women according to the knowledge of family planning methods*

Knowledge & Use of contraceptives	*Hindu*	*Muslim*
Knowledge of any method	**98.4 (241)**	**93.4 (241)**
Female Sterilisation	76.3 (187)	69.0 (178)
Male Sterilisation	65.3 (160)	54.3 (140)
Copper-T	80.0 (196)	56.2 (145)
Oral Pills	85.3 (209)	77.9 (201)
Condom	93.1 (228)	80.6 (208)
Rhythmic/Periodic Abstinence	58.4 (143)	43.0 (111)
Withdrawal Method	48.2 (118)	31.8 (82)
Others	8.6 (21)	4.7 (12)
Use of Any Method	**52.7 (119)**	**36.0 (85)**
Female Sterilisation	15.1 (18)	12.9 (11)
Male Sterilisation	4.2 (5)	4.7 (4)
Copper-T	6.7 (8)	7.1 (6)
Oral Pills	37.8 (45)	43.5 (37)
Condom	26.9 (32)	20.0 (17)
Rhythmic/Periodic Abstinence	5.9 (7)	4.7 (4)
Withdrawal Method	3.4 (4)	5.9 (5)
Others	—	1.2 (1)

* Multiple responses.
Note : Figures in parentheses indicate the absolute number.
Source : Field data.

As far as the use of contraceptives is concerned, only 52.7 per cent and 36.0 per cent of the Hindu and Muslim women respectively are found using family planning methods. Among the different methods, the oral pills and female sterilisation were the most commonly used methods by the sample respondents. For instance, 37.8 per cent of the Hindu women and 43.5 per cent of the Muslim women have been found using oral pills. Condom is used by 26.9 per cent and 20.0 per cent of the Hindu and Muslim women respectively. Female sterilisation is the third most popular choice amongst the current users of family planning methods amongst both Hindu and Muslim women. However, the use of male sterilisation and copper-T as well as the traditional methods has been found low.

The findings of the present study approximate the findings of the NFHS-II for Assam. As according to the NFHS-II, 1998-99, the percentages of the Hindu and Muslim couples of reproductive ages practising contraception stood at 49 per cent and 34 per cent respectively (Kulkarni and Alagarajan, 2005). The data on current use of contraception from the present study and the NFHS-II have been presented in the Figure 4.1.

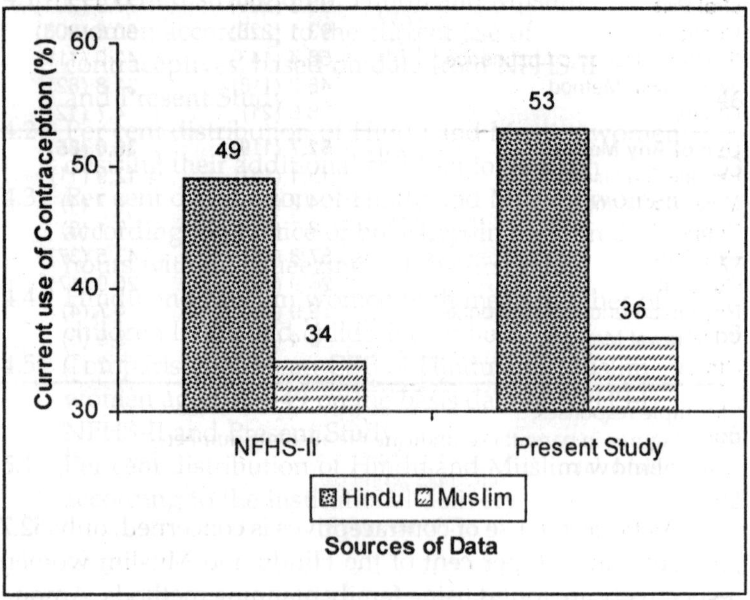

Fig. 4.1: Per cent distribution of Hindu and Muslim women according to the current use of contraceptives, based on data from NFHS-II and Present Study

Current use of contraception by selected background characteristics

As Table 4.2 suggests, the current age of the women hardly exerts any influence on the current use of contraception, though the use of contraception among the younger Muslim women in the age group of 15-24 is found higher (36.0 per cent) than the older women in the age group of 35-49 (i.e. 29.9 per cent).

There is observed marked variation in the current use of contraception when the women are analysed by their age at marriage. For instance, 54.9 per cent and 43.6 per cent of the Hindu and Muslim women respectively are found using contraception who got married after the age of 18 as compared to 43.2 per cent and 28.6 per cent respectively who got married before the age of 18. The higher use among the married women may be attributed to higher education that the women in probability had got and, hence, they got married at higher ages.

Table 4.2: Per cent distribution of the Hindu and Muslim women according to the current use of family planning methods by selected background variables

Background variables	*Hindu*	*Muslim*
Current age of the women		
15-24	55.9 (19)	36.0 (18)
25-34	52.0 (64)	39.5 (47)
35-49	52.2 (36)	29.9 (20)
Age at marriage		
Below 18 years	43.2 (19)	28.6 (34)
After 18 years	54.9 (100)	43.6 (51)
Type of family		
Nuclear	58.1 (86)	36.8 (63)
Joint	42.3 (33)	33.8 (22)
Women's education		
Illiterate	22.2 (6)	20.7 (18)
Less than middle school	53.8 (43)	46.0 (46)
Middle school and above	56.9 (70)	47.7 (21)
Media exposure		
Low	51.0 (26)	29.0 (31)
Medium	51.5 (69)	40.4 (46)
High	58.5 (24)	53.3 (8)
Standard of living		
Low	47.4 (45)	28.6 (42)
High	56.5 (74)	48.3 (43)

Note: Figures in the parentheses represent absolute number.
Source: Field data.

Type of family in which the women live also seems to have influence on the current use of contraception. The women living in the nuclear family are using more contraception than the women living in joint family. For example, 58.1 per cent of the Hindu women and 36.8 per cent of the Muslim women living in nuclear family are using contraception compared to 42.3 per cent of the Hindu women and 33.8 per cent of the Muslim women living in the joint family.

The current use of contraception is positively associated with the education of the women, education of the husband and the standard of living. Lastly, the percentage of contraception use is found to be higher among the Hindu and Muslim women having high media exposure.

Main reason of non-use of contraception

The women have forwarded varied reasons for not using contraception. 'Health problems' has been cited by 26.1 per cent of the Hindu women as the main reason for not using contraception. However, 21.2 per cent of the Muslim women cited 'Want children' as the main reason. The percentage of Hindu women citing the reason 'Want children' is 16.2 per cent and the percentage of Muslim citing 'Health problems' as the main reason of non-use of contraception is 13.7 per cent. The other main reasons for non-use for both Hindu and Muslim women are presented in Table 4.3.

Table 4.3: Per cent distribution of the Hindu and Muslim women according to the main reason of not using family planning methods

Reasons	*Hindu*	*Muslim*
Hard to get	5.4 (6)	5.5 (8)
Health problems	26.1 (29)	13.7 (20)
Cost too much	5.4 (6)	8.2 (12)
Against Religion	3.6 (4)	14.4 (21)
Not having sex/infrequent sex	9.0 (10)	9.6 (14)
Husband away/separated	13.5 (15)	13.0 (19)
Breastfeeding/postpartum	15.3 (17)	7.5 (11)
Afraid of sterilisation	5.4 (6)	6.8 (10)
Want Children	16.2 (18)	21.2 (31)

Note: Figures in the parentheses represent absolute number.
Source: Field data.

Determinants of contraceptive use: Results of logistic regression analysis

As shown in Table 4.4, all the independent variables used in the model were found significantly affecting the contraceptive use of the women. But once the other variables were adjusted in the model to see the effect of one independent variable on the dependent variable, only three variables, namely type of the family, women's education and the standard of living remained as significant variables affecting the contraceptive use.

Table 4.4: Results of logistic regression analyses showing the impact of selected background variables on the current contraceptive use before and after the adjustment of other variables

Variables	*Before adjustment* Exp (β)	*After adjustment* Exp (β)
Religion (rc: Hindu)		
Muslim	0.5***	0.8
Age at marriage (rc: Below 18 years)		
After 18 years	2.2***	1.2
No. of children living (rc: less than 2)		
More than 2	0.5***	0.9
Place of Current Residence (rc: Rural)		
Urban	1.4*	0.9
Type of Family (rc: Nuclear)		
Joint	0.7*	0.6**
Women's Education (rc: Illiterate)		
Less than middle school	3.7***	3.0***
Middle school & above	4.5***	2.6***
Standard of living (rc: low)		
High	2.1***	1.5*

Note: *** Significant at 1 per cent level
** Significant at 5 per cent level
* Significant at 10 per cent level
The remaining variables acted as the control variables for the particular independent variable in question in the model. The two codes of the dependent variable (i.e. contraceptive use) used in the model are 'Not using' (Code = 0) and 'Using' (Code = 1).

For instance, the results suggest that the women living in the joint family are less likely to use contraceptive than the women living in the nuclear family with Exp (β) of 0.6. However, the women with education level of less than middle school and more than middle school are 3.0 times and 2.6 times more likely to use contraceptive than the illiterate women. Likewise, the women with high standard of living are 1.5 times more likely to use contraceptives than the women having low standard of living.

As far as religion is concerned, before the adjustment of the background variables, it acted as a significant variable with the finding that the Muslim women are less likely to use contraceptive than the Hindu women. But as soon as the other variables are taken into account in the model, religion loses its statistical significance as an explanatory variable of contraceptive use.

Fertility Preferences

It is often said that data on fertility preferences may be misleading, because : first, attitudes towards childbearing may not be fully formed and they may change over time and second, the responses may not take into account the effect of social pressures or the attitudes of the husband and other family members, who may have major influence on reproductive decisions. Nevertheless, the data on desire for additional children can be useful as a crude indicator of general attitudes and the future course of fertility (NFHS, 1991-92, Assam).

Several social scientists recognize India as strong patrilineal society and there are several stereotypes in the Indian society. A popular stereotype is the strong preference for male child (Nath and Land, 1994). Many other studies have also substantiated this fact (Williamson, 1976; Cleland *et al.*, 1983; Mason, 1992; Rahman and DaVanzo, 1993; Nath and Goswami, 1997; Nath and Leonetti, 2001; and Nath and Deka, 2004). Son preference is generally regarded as an important factor influencing fertility decisions. The practice of dowry and importance of sons for religious rites mean Hindus have stronger preference for sons than Muslims (Bhat and Zavier, 2005).

Desire for additional children and the background characteristics

The data presented in Table 4.5 show that 41.2 per cent and 45.3 per cent of the Hindu and Muslim women respectively desire to have another children in future.

When we look at the women by their current age, then we see that the desire for additional children decreases with the increase in the age. This is quite natural too for the women to have lesser desire for children at higher ages.

Table 4.5: Per cent distribution of the Hindu and Muslim women according to the desire for additional children by background characteristics

Background characteristics	*Hindu*	*Muslim*
Current age of women		
15-24	70.3 (26)	75.4 (43)
25-34	46.7 (63)	45.8 (60)
35-49	16.4 (12)	20.0 (14)
No. of living children		
≤ 2	54.3 (94)	66.1 (82)
≥ 3	9.7 (7)	26.1 (35)
Desire for additional children	**41.2 (101)**	**45.3 (117)**

Note: Figures in the parentheses represent absolute number.
Source: Field data.

Likewise, the desire for additional children goes down with increase in the number of children living. For example, as compared to 54.3 per cent of the Hindu women with 2 or less than 2 children desiring for additional children, only 9.7 per cent of them with 3 or more than 3 children desire additional children. Likewise, 26.1 per cent of the Muslim women with 3 or more children desire additional children as compared to 66.1 per cent of the Muslim women desiring additional children with 2 or less than 2 children.

Son preference and the background characteristics

Table 4.6 presents the data on son preference of the women along with the data on son preference by some selected background characteristics. Out of those who want to have children in future, 61.4 per cent of the Hindu women's preferred sex of the additional child is that of male, whereas the corresponding figure for the Muslim women is 53 per cent (Figure 4.2). It can, therefore, be safely said that son preference is high in both Hindu and Muslim communities, though higher among the Hindus.

Table 4.6: Per cent distribution of the Hindu and Muslim women according to the son preference by selected background variables

Background variables	*Hindu*	*Muslim*
Current age of the women		
15-24	53.8 (14)	58.1 (25)
25-34	61.9 (39)	48.3 (29)
35-49	75.0 (9)	57.1 (8)
No. of children living		
≤ 2	59.6 (56)	51.2 (42)
≥ 3	85.7 (6)	57.1 (20)
Place of residence		
Rural	73.5 (36)	53.2 (41)
Urban	50.0 (26)	52.5 (21)
Type of family		
Nuclear	64.2 (43)	51.1 (46)
Joint	55.9 (19)	59.3 (16)
Women's education		
Illiterate	42.9 (3)	58.5 (24)
Less than middle school	72.5 (29)	51.9 (28)
Middle school and above	55.6 (30)	45.5 (10)
Husband's education		
Illiterate	100.0 (4)	69.2 (27)
Less than middle school	61.8 (21)	46.7 (21)
Middle school and above	58.7 (37)	42.4 (14)
Standard of living		
Low	66.7 (28)	59.4 (41)
High	57.6 (34)	43.8 (21)
Son preference	**61.4 (62)**	**53.0 (62)**

Note: Figures in the parentheses represent absolute number.
Source: Field data.

The son preference is found to be high among the aged women, women with 3 or more living children, rural women, women whose husbands are illiterate and women with low standard of living.

The son preference is found higher among the Hindu women living in nuclear family. However, for the Muslim women, the desire for son is found higher among the women living in joint family. As far as the women's education is concerned, the son preference exists among the women of all three educational categories. However, it is the highest among the Hindu women who are literate but have not completed the middle school, but it is the illiterate Muslim women who show the highest degree of son preference.

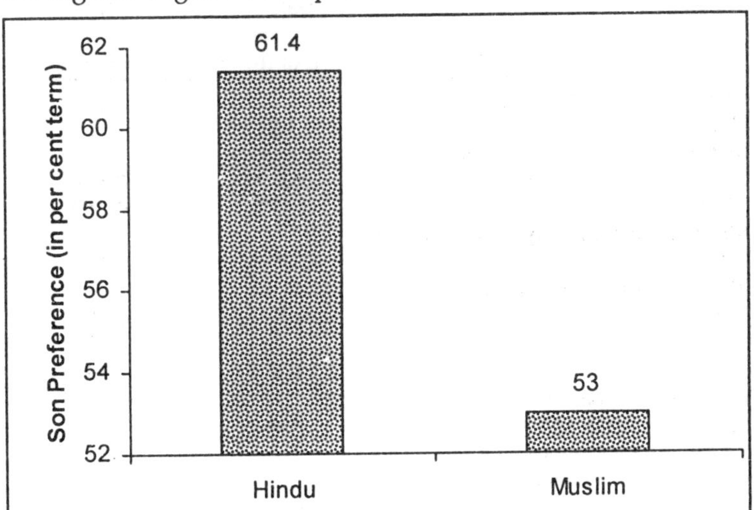

Fig 4.2: Per cent distribution of Hindu and Muslim women desiring their additional children to be a son

Determinants of desire for additional children: Results of logistic regression analyses

In the following logistic regression analysis model, altogether nine variables were entered to see their effect on the dependent variable, namely desire for additional children. The results so derived are presented in Table 4.7, which shows that the Muslim women are 1.6 times more likely to desire for additional children as compared to the Hindu women after the control of the background variables. However, when religion is considered in the model as the only explanatory variable, it is not found as a significant variable influencing the desire for additional children of the women.

Table 4.7: Results of logistic regression analyses showing the impact of selected background variables on the desire for additional children before and after the adjustment of other variables

Variables	*Before adjustment* Exp (β)	*After adjustment* Exp (β)
Religion (rc: Hindu)		
Muslim	1.2	1.6*
Current age (rc: 15 - 24 years)		
35-34	0.3***	0.5***
35-49	0.1***	0.2***
No. of children living (rc: less than 2)		
More than 2	0.2***	0.1***
Place of Current Residence (rc: Rural)		
Urban	0.7**	0.5***
Type of Family (rc: Nuclear)		
Joint	0.8	0.9
Women's Education (rc: Illiterate)		
Less than middle school	1.4	0.9
Middle school & above	1.2	0.8
Work status of women (rc: Not working)		
Working	0.5**	0.5*

Note: *** Significant at 1 per cent level
** Significant at 5 per cent level
* Significant at 10 per cent level
The remaining variables acted as the control variables for the particular independent variable in question in the model. The two codes of the dependent variable (i.e. desire for additional children) used in the model are 'No' (Code = 0) and 'Yes' (Code = 1)

As far as the current age is concerned, it is found that the aged women's desire for additional children is lower than the younger women. Similarly the women with more than 2 children are less likely to desire additional children than the women with 2 or less than 2 children.

Likewise, the urban women's and the working women's desire for additional children are likely to be lesser than the rural women {Exp (β) = 0.5} and non-working women {Exp (β) = 0.5} respectively.

The type of the family in which the women live and the education level of the women are not found statistically significant explanatory variable affecting desire for additional children of the women.

Breastfeeding

Breastfeeding is considered very important for the health of the infants. Beneficial effects of breastfeeding on infant health and survival are well known (Krishnamoorthy and Sheela, 2004). Breastfeeding improves the nutritional status of young children and reduces morbidity and mortality. Breast milk not only provides the child with important nutrients but also protects the child against certain infections. For the mother, as soon as the infant starts suckling at the breast, the hormone oxytocin is released, resulting in uterine contractions of the mother that reduce the risk of postpartum haemorrhage and facilitate the expulsion of the placenta. Therefore, it is medically recommended that the first breast milk should be given to the child rather than squeezed out from the breast because the first milk contains colostrum, which provides natural immunity to the child. Therefore, early initiation of breastfeeding without squeezing out the first milk is very important because it benefits both the mother and the infant (NFHS 1992-93).

Past studies (IIPS, 1995; IIPS and ORC Macro, 2000; Khan, 1990; Krishnamoorthy, 1970; Padmini and Krishnamoorthy, 1988; and Krishnamoorthy and Sheela, 2004) showed that the socio-economic factors have strong effect on the initiation and duration of breastfeeding.

Basic breastfeeaing information

As far as the overall breastfeeding is concerned (Table 4.8), among the Hindu women (214) and Muslim women (213) who gave live births during the five years period preceding the survey, altogether 98.1 per cent of the Hindu women and 97.2 per cent of the Muslim women have been found to have breastfed their newborn babies. So breastfeeding practice is quite common amongst both Hindu and Muslim women.

Regarding the timing of breastfeeding, it has been found that 46.7 per cent of the Hindu women and 36.2 per cent of the Muslim women breastfed their child within 2 hours of birth. Then 28.6 per cent and 33.8 per cent of the Hindu and Muslim women respectively breastfed their child on the same day but after 2 hours of birth only. The rest of the women—both Hindu and Muslim—breastfed their babies afterwards.

Table 4.8: Basic breastfeeding information of the Hindu and Muslim women who gave birth during the 5 years period preceding the survey

Breastfeeding Information	*Hindu*	*Muslim*
Percentage that breastfed	98.1 (210)	97.2 (207)
Timing of breastfeeding		
Within 2 hours of birth	46.7 (98)	36.2 (75)
After 2 hours of birth	28.6 (60)	33.8 (70)
Next day and afterwards	24.8 (52)	30.0 (62)
Percentage that breastfed after squeezing out the first milk	40.0 (84)	33.8 (70)

But those Hindu and Muslim women who breastfed their newborn, 40.0 per cent and 33.8 per cent of them squeezed out the first milk from their breast before giving milk to the babies (Figure 4.3). However, it is medically recommended that the first breast milk should be given to the child rather than squeezed out from the breast because the first milk contains colostrums, which provides natural immunity to the child.

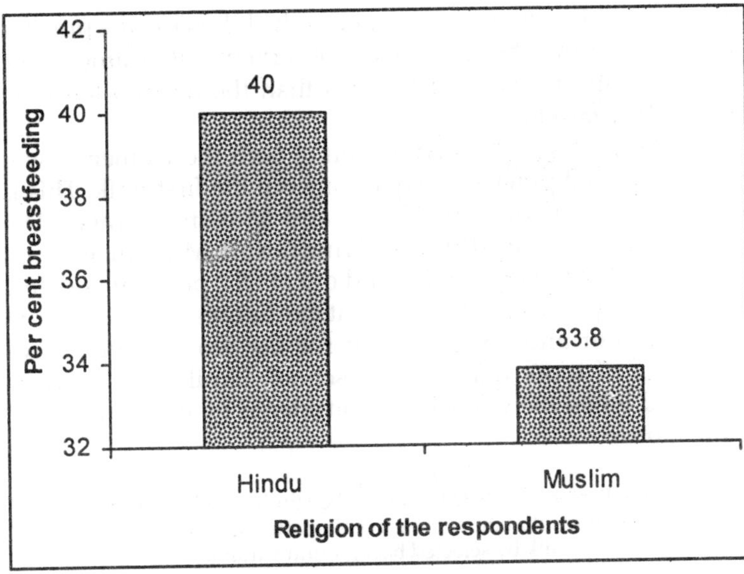

Fig 4.3: Per cent distribution of Hindu and Muslim women according to practice of breastfeeding within 2 hours without squeezing out the first milk

Breastfeeding by background characteristics

Table 4.9 provides information about the initiation of breastfeeding after squeezing out the first milk by selected background characteristics. It is the older women, i.e. in the age group of 35-49 who mainly tend to squeeze out the first milk. For example, 48.9 per cent of the Hindu women and 39.5 per cent of the Muslim women in the age group of 35-49 squeezed out the first milk as compared to 34.6 per cent of the Hindu women and 31.0 per cent of the Muslim women in the age group of 24-35. The respective percentages of the Hindu and Muslim women breastfeeding in the above way in the age group of 15-24 are estimated at 47.2 per cent and 35.8 per cent respectively.

From the place of residence point of view, rural women follow the practice of squeezing out the first milk more than the urban women. For instance, 43.0 per cent and 35.3 per cent of the rural Hindu and Muslim women squeezed out the first milk as compared to 36.9 per cent and 31.9 per cent of the urban

Hindu and Muslim women respectively. Likewise, the practice of squeezing out the first milk is observed higher among the women living in the joint families than the women living in the nuclear families.

Higher the level of education of both the women, lower is the observed practice of squeezing out the first milk. This is observed valid for both Hindu and Muslim women. The percentages of the illiterate Hindu and Muslim women squeezing out the first milk stand out at 68.0 per cent and 46.2 per cent respectively. The percentage figures come down to 24.8 per cent and 25.6 per cent for the women who have schooling of more than middle school. Similar is the trend observed when the women are considered by their husbands' education.

Table 4.9: Percentage distribution of the Hindu and Muslim women according to the initiation of breastfeeding after squeezing out the first milk by selected background variables

Background variables	***Breastfeeding after squeezing out the first milk***	
	Hindu	***Muslim***
Age of the women		
15-24	47.2 (17)	35.8 (19)
25-34	34.6 (44)	31.0 (36)
35-49	48.9 (23)	39.5 (15)
Place of current residence		
Rural	43.0 (46)	35.3 (41)
Urban	36.9 (38)	31.9 (29)
Type of the family		
Nuclear	39.3 (55)	33.3 (51)
Joint	41.4 (29)	35.2 (19)
Education of the women		
Illiterate	68.0 (17)	46.2 (36)
Less than middle school	52.6 (40)	28.1 (27)
More than middle school	24.8 (27)	25.6 (10)
Husband's education		
Illiterate	70.6 (12)	44.8 (30)
Less than middle school	55.6 (35)	29.8 (25)
More than middle school	28.2 (35)	28.0 (14)
Standard of living		
Low	53.7 (51)	41.7 (55)
High	28.7 (33)	20.0 (15)

Note: Figures in the parentheses represent absolute number.
Source: Field data.

Likewise, it has been seen that as the standard of living of the women goes up, the practice of squeezing out the first milk goes down. That is why when the standard of living goes up from low to high, the unhealthy practice of squeezing out the first milk goes down from 53.7 per cent to 28.7 per cent for the Hindu women and from 41.7 per cent to 20.0 per cent for the Muslim women.

Determinants of breastfeeding practice: Results of logistic regression analyses

In the following logistic regression model, altogether six (6) independent variables are entered to see their effect on the dependent variable, namely the breastfeeding practice.

The results show that (Table 4.10) when the other background variables are not adjusted in the model, women's

Table 4.10: Results of logistic regression analyses showing the impact of selected background variables on the breastfeeding practice with and without squeezing out the first milk before and after the adjustment of other variables

Variables	*Before adjustment* Exp (β)	*After adjustment* Exp (β)
Religion (rc: Hindu)		
Muslim	0.8	0.4***
Current age (rc: 15-24 years)		
35-34	0.7	0.8
35-49	1.2	1.1
Place of Current Residence (rc: Rural)		
Urban	0.8	1.7**
Women's Education (rc: Illiterate)		
Less than middle school	0.6**	0.7
Middle school & above	0.3***	0.4**
Place of delivery (rc: Home)		
Institution	0.4***	0.5***
Standard of living (rc: Low)		
High	0.4***	0.5**

Note: *** Significant at 1 per cent level
** Significant at 5 per cent level
* Significant at 10 per cent level
The remaining variables acted as the control variables for the particular independent variable in question in the model. The two codes of the dependent variable (i.e. contraceptive use) used in the model are 'Did not squeeze out' (Code = 0) and 'Squeezed out' (Code = 1).

education, place of delivery and standard of living are found to affect breastfeeding practice of the women significantly. In all these cases it is found that the women who are literates, whose child delivery took place in medical institution and have high standard of living are less likely to squeeze out the first milk in comparison to their respective reference categories.

After the control of the background variables, religion and current place of residence also become significant exploratory variables affecting the breastfeeding practice of the women, along with the variables mentioned just above. Except the current place of residence, in case of all other independent variables, women are found less likely to squeeze out the first milk in comparison to their respective reference categories. In the case of current place of residence, the probability of urban women squeezing out the first milk is 1.7 times higher than the rural women.

Outcome of Pregnancies of Ever-married Women

Experts say that it is always very difficult to collect retrospective information on pregnancies than on live births, particularly on pregnancies spontaneously aborted within the first few months of conception. The total number of pregnancies and the percentage of all pregnancies that end in spontaneous abortions are more likely to be under-estimated. Stillbirths are probably much more accurately reported than abortions.

James and Nair (2005) observed that abortion is not widely practiced in India as a mechanism of fertility control given the cultural ethos of different religious communities. However, in recent years, there has been emerging concern about the practice of induced abortion as a mechanism for having male children and avoiding the delivery of the girl child.

The fact remains that there is no conclusive evidence yet from any parts of the country to substantiate widespread practice of induced abortions. Quite often, the respondents may suppress the information on induced abortions, or induced abortions may be reported as spontaneous abortions. Therefore, these data should not be subject to very intensive interpretation (NFHS, 1992-93).

Outcome of pregnancies—spontaneous abortion, induced abortion, stillbirth and live birth

Out of the total 220 last pregnancies that the Hindu women had during the 5 years period preceding the survey, 97.3 per cent of them culminated in live births (Table 4.11). Likewise, 95.1 per cent of the last pregnancies of 224 Muslim women ended up with live births.

Only 0.5 per cent and 1.3 per cent of the last pregnancies of the Hindu and Muslim women respectively ended up with spontaneous. Induced abortion accounted for 1.8 per cent of last pregnancies of Muslim women, whereas none of the Hindu women went for induced abortion. Lastly, 2.3 per cent and 1.8 per cent of the Hindu and Muslim women respectively had the outcome of stillbirth of their last pregnancies

Table 4.11: Per cent distribution of ever-married Hindu and Muslim women by the outcome of the last pregnancy occurring during the 5 years period preceding the survey

Outcome of the pregnancies	*Hindu*	*Muslim*
Live birth	97.3	95.1
Spontaneous abortion	0.5	1.3
Induced abortion	—	1.8
Stillbir.h	2.3	1.8
Total per cent	100.0 (220)	100.0 (224)

Note: Figures in the parentheses represent number of pregnancies.
Source: Field data.

Hence, it can be concluded that more or less same percentages of the Hindu and Muslim pregnancies ended up with live births, with stillbirth accounting for next highest outcome of the all last pregnancies occurring during the 5 years period preceding the survey.

Fertility

In the present study, the fertility of the Hindu and Muslim women has been measured in terms of the mean number of children ever born and mean number of children living. To measure the mean number of children living, the children whom the woman has given birth and presently living as well as not living with her included.

Hindu-Muslim differentials in mean number of children ever born and mean number of children living

Many studies have shown that the number of children ever born or children living varies significantly between the Hindu and Muslim women in India. According to the National Family Health Survey, 1992-93 and 1998-99, Assam, Hindu-Muslim differential in fertility exists in Assam too.

Table 4.12: Mean number of children living and mean CEB of the Hindu and Muslim women aged 15-49

Fertility	*Hindu*	*Muslim*
Mean Number of children living	2.1 (1.07)	2.9 (1.15)
Mean CEB	2.2 (1.15)	3.2 (1.84)

Note: Figures in the parentheses represent standard deviation.
Source: Field data.

In the present study also, the mean number of children living and mean number of children ever born are found higher for Muslim women than the Hindu women (Table 4.12). For example, Hindu women's mean number of children living is estimated at 2.1, whereas the corresponding figure for the Muslim women is estimated to be 2.9 children. Likewise, the mean children ever born for the Hindu woman is found out to be 2.2 in comparison to 3.2 of the Muslim women (Figure 4.4). These differences in the mean CEB and mean children living are found to be statistically significant at 1 per cent level.

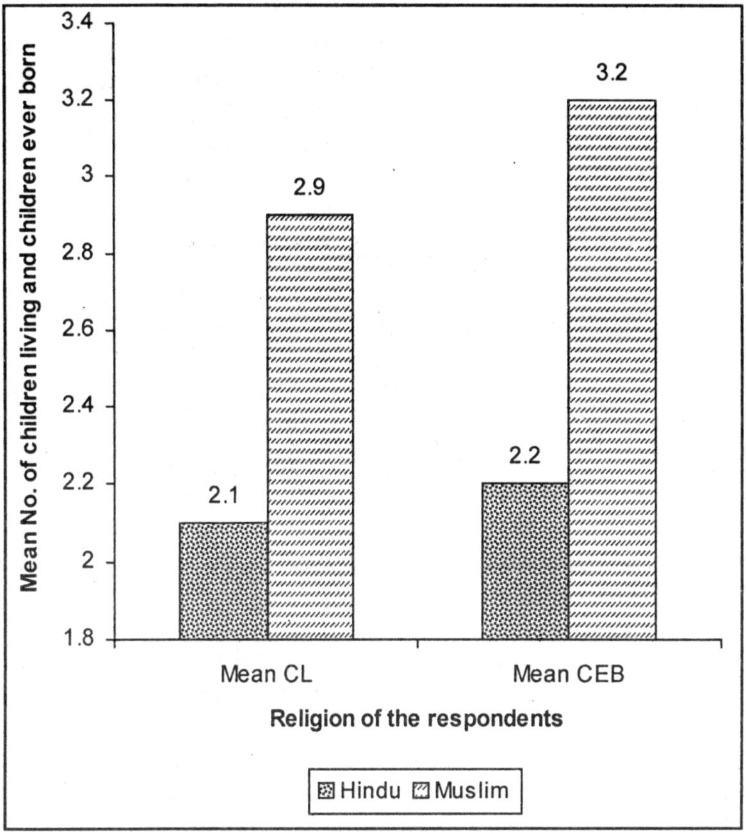

Fig 4.4: Hindu and Muslim women with mean number of children living and children ever born

Distribution of Hindu-Muslim women according to the number of children living

Table 4.13 presents data on percentage distribution of the Hindu and Muslim women according to the number of children living. The percentage of women with 2 or less than 2 living children is found to be higher among the Hindus than the Muslims. For example, 33.1 per cent of the Hindu women are found to have 1 living child, whereas the respective figure for the Muslim women is 20.9 per cent. Likewise, 37.6 per cent of the Hindu women have been found to have 2 living children as against 27.1 per cent of the Muslim women. In totality, 70.7 per cent of the Hindu women have 2 or less than 2 children, while the corresponding figure for the Muslim women is 48.0 per cent.

Table 4.13: Per cent distribution of ever-married Hindu and Muslim women according to the number of children living

No. of children living	*Hindu*	*Muslim*
1	33.1	20.9
2	37.6	27.1
3	18.0	20.2
4	7.8	13.6
5	3.7	18.2

Source: Field data.

On the other hand, larger proportions of the Muslim women have higher order birth. For instance, 20.2 per cent of the Muslim women have 3 children as compared to 18.0 per cent of the Hindu women. Likewise, higher percentages of Muslim women are found to have 4 and 5 + children compared to their Hindu counterparts. In totality, 52 per cent of Muslim women are found to have 3 or more than 3 children as compared to 29.5 per cent of the Hindu women.

Comparison with the NFHS-I and NFHS-II fertility data

A comparison of the mean children ever born to women of age 40-49 of the present study and that of the NFHS-I (1992-93) and NFHS-II (1998-99) is presented in Table 4.14. The mean CEB of women aged 40-49 is chosen for comparison because it measures the completed fertility of the cohort of women who are near the end of the childbearing span at the time of the survey since the fertility beyond the age of 40 is quite low.

However, during the comparison of the CEB of the women aged 40-49, it must be kept in mind that data in the present study relate to the Sonitpur district of Assam only, whereas NFHS-I and NFHS-II data relate to the entire state.

Table 4.14: Mean children ever born to Hindu and Muslim women aged 40-49 from the present study (Sonitpur district), NFHS-I (Assam) and NFHS-II (Assam)

Sources of data	*Hindu*	*Muslim*
NFHS-I (1992-93)	5.4	6.7
NFHS-II (1998-99)	4.0	5.3
Present Study (2002-03)	2.9	5.6

Source: Field data and Reports of NFHS-I and NFHS-II on Assam.

Table 4.15 highlights the fact that the fertility, measured in terms of mean CEB, of both Hindus and Muslims has declined between 1992-93 and 2006. Between NFHS-I and NFHS-II, the mean CEB of the Hindu women came down by 1.4 children and that of the Muslim women by 1.4 children. But the fact remains that the fertility of the Muslims was higher than the Hindus in both NFHS surveys.

When the mean CEB of the present study is compared with the NFHS-II data, it is seen that the mean CEB of the Hindu women comes down from 4.0 to 2.9 in the present study. On the other hand, the mean CEB of the Muslim women in the present study comes out to be 5.6 children in comparison to the mean CEB of 5.3 children in the NFHS-II. The gap between the Hindu-Muslim fertility in NFHS-II stood at 1.3 children, whereas the present study shows the gap at 2.7 children. The comparative Hindu-Muslim fertility, as measured by the above-mentioned three studies, is shown in the Figure 4.5.

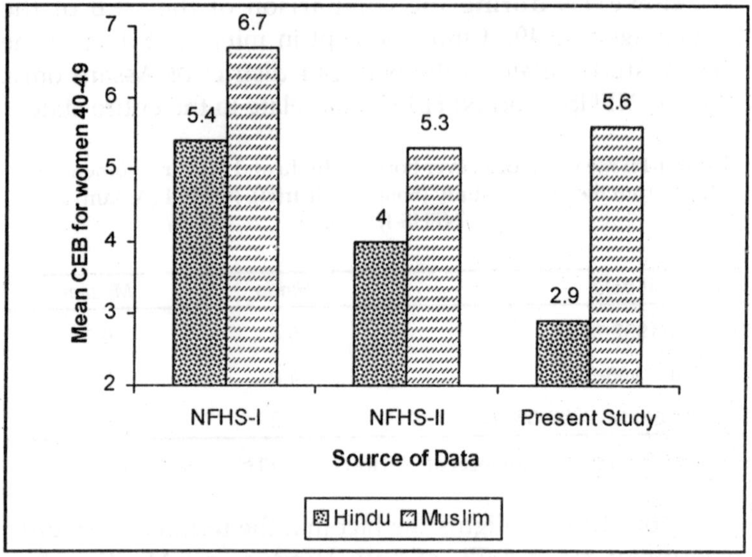

Fig 4.5: Comparison of Mean CEB of Hindu and Muslim women aged 40–49 on the basis data of NFHS-I, NFHS-II and Present Study

Socio-economic correlates of fertility

Population scientists claim that the background socio-economic characteristics of the women have important bearing on their fertility. For example, the women who are educated, whose husbands are also educated, who live in the urban area, who are working, etc. have lower fertility than those whose spouses are uneducated, live in rural area, do not work outside home, etc. In this section, the mean number of children living to Hindu and Muslim women are examined by their selected background characteristics (Table 4.15).

Current age group of the women

It has been well documented that the fertility of women is closely related with the women's age. This is because older women complete longer reproductive life span than the younger women. This, in turn, affects their overall fertility.

Table 4.15: Mean number of children living to the Hindu and Muslim women according to the current age of the women

Variable	*Hindu*		*Muslim*	
	Mean	SD	Mean	SD
Current age of the women				
15-24	1.4 (32)	0.60	1.9 (107)	0.93
25-34	2.0 (266)	1.01	2.8 (370)	1.43
35-49	2.7 (199)	1.07	4.0 (278)	1.79
Age at marriage				
Before 18 years	2.6 (131)	1.14	3.6 (466)	1.65
After 18 years	2.0 (387)	1.01	2.2 (289)	1.27
Place of residence				
Rural	2.4 (290)	1.13	3.1 (431)	1.59
Urban	1.9 (228)	0.94	2.8 (324)	1.65
Type of family				
Nuclear	2.0 (324)	0.97	2.9 (547)	1.62
Joint	2.3 (194)	1.22	3.1 (208)	1.62
Education of the women				
Illiterate	2.9 (80)	1.18	3.7 (355)	1.66
Less than middle school	2.3 (196)	1.17	2.8 (308)	1.54
Middle school +	1.9 (242)	0.87	1.9 (92)	0.88
Work status of the women				
Working	2.1 (455)	1.09	2.9 (706)	1.64
Not working	1.8 (63)	0.93	2.9 (49)	1.32
Education of the husband				
Illiterate	2.7 (51)	1.06	3.6 (288)	1.66
Less than middle school	2.3 (171)	1.15	3.0 (313)	1.61
Middle school +	1.9 (270)	0.94	2.0 (122)	1.02
Husband's occupation				
Agriculture/Farming	2.8 (110)	1.14	4.1 (69)	1.64
Service	1.8 (149)	0.86	1.8 (42)	0.94
Business	1.9 (150)	0.95	2.8 (402)	1.57
Others	2.5 (83)	1.09	3.2 (210)	1.64
Standard of living				
Low	2.4 (259)	1.20	3.4 (537)	1.59
High	1.9 (259)	0.89	2.2 (218)	1.43
Ever use of contraceptive				
No	2.3 (272)	1.23	3.2 (518)	1.69
Yes	1.9 (246)	0.86	2.5 (237)	1.41
Experience of child loss				
No	2.1 (459)	1.05	2.8 (582)	1.60
Yes	2.4 (59)	1.22	3.5 (183)	1.61
Exposure to the media				
Low	2.2 (119)	1.11	3.2 (372)	1.69
Medium	2.2 (316)	1.09	2.6 (353)	1.57
High	1.8 (83)	0.93	1.8 (30)	0.75

Source: Field data.

Therefore, it is expected that younger women would have lesser number of children living than their elderly counterpart.

The present study reveals that the mean number of children living has a positive association with the age of the women. The mean number of children living to the Hindu women in the age group of 35-49 is 2.7 as compared to 1.4 for the women in the age group of 15-24. Likewise, the mean number of children living to the Muslim women aged 35-49 is 4.0 and the corresponding figure for the women aged 15-24 is 1.9. Comparatively, the difference of children between the Hindu women in the age groups of 15-24 and 35-49 is found to be 1.3, while the corresponding difference for the Muslim women is figured out at 2.1.

Age at marriage of the women

Female age at marriage acts as an important factor determining the fertility. The impact of this factor on fertility is more evident in societies where the use of contraception is very low. This is because the age at marriage is a prime factor determining the reproductive life span of a woman. Higher the age at marriage, lower is the reproductive life span of the woman. Studies (Smith, 1980: Reddy, 1986) have shown that an increase in the age at marriage can lead to decline in the fertility rate of the women.

Both Hindu and Muslim women who married before the age of 18 years have higher mean number of children living than the women married after the age of 18. For example, the mean number of children living for the Hindu women married after the age 18 is more or less the same, i.e. 2.0 children for the Hindu women against the 2.2 children for the Muslim women. However, the mean number of children living differs widely between the Hindu and Muslim women who got married before the age of 18. The mean number of children living is 2.6 for Hindu women and 3.6 for the Muslim women getting married before the age of 18 years and, hence, showing a difference of one children between the Hindu and Muslim women.

Place of current residence

Place of residence is another variable that has influence on fertility behaviour of the women (Shrivastava, 1996; Raj, 1996). Urban women's greater exposure to education and modern values that favour late marriage and the greater distance from the community and family based social control has definite impact on fertility. Therefore, it can be expected that urban women will have lower fertility than the rural women.

Table 4.15 shows that the mean number of children living is indeed lower in the urban area (i.e. 1.9) than in the rural area (i.e. 2.4) for the Hindu women. Likewise, the mean number of children living of 3.1 for the rural Muslim women is higher than the urban Muslim women's mean number of children living of 2.8.

Type of the family

The type of family in which the woman lives may also have impact on her fertility behaviour. The desire to have a certain number of children is an intra-familial decision. Nuclear and child centred families have fewer children (Shrivastava, 1996; Raj, 1996). In Indian culture, therefore, it can be expected that the familial and societal influences as well as lesser financial liability in a joint family system may lead to higher fertility.

The association between the type of the family and the women's fertility has been found in the expected direction for the Hindu and Muslim women. The mean number of children living for the Hindu and Muslim women in nuclear families stands at 2.0 and 2.9 respectively, compared to the figures of 2.3 and 3.1 for the Hindu and Muslim women living in joint families.

Education of the women

Education is an important indicator relevant for any kind of fertility analysis. Since the formulation of the demographic transition theory, education has quite often been used as an indicator to measure socio-economic development in different societies (UN, 1995). Many studies have substantiated the negative relationship that exists between female education and fertility.

In Indian context, however, the overall effect of the inverse relationship between education and fertility is not found as strong as in developed countries (UN, 1993). However, in developing countries like India, there appears to be a high threshold level of education beyond which only marked differentials in fertility are generated (Moulasha, 2000).

It can be seen from the above table that the mean number of children living declines steadily with the increase in the education level of both the Hindu and Muslim women. The mean number of children living is 2.9 and 3.7 respectively to illiterate Hindu and Muslim women as compared to the corresponding figure of 1.9 for both Hindu and Muslim women who have studied beyond middle school level.

Work status of the women

Women's work status has been used by many demographers as an indicator to explain fertility differentials among different groups of population. In developed countries, the work participation and fertility have shown negative association. However, researchers have come out with conflicting results about the effect of women's work participation on fertility. It may be possible that women take up employment in order to reduce the economic burden caused by high fertility. In such a situation women's work status and their fertility performance may be poorly correlated or even positive (Kumar, 1997). Some population scientists believe that the commonly observed relationship between work participation and fertility in a population is spurious and there are other factors that may influence the fertility levels among working and non-working women (Terry, 1975).

The present study shows that both working and non-working Muslim women have the same mean number of children living. However, the mean number of children living for the working and non-working Hindu women varies slightly with 2.1 children for the non-working women and 1.8 children for the working women.

Education of the husband

Women's fertility is undoubtedly affected by their husbands' characteristics, notably, husband's education, occupation and family income (UN, 1987). Like the women's education, husband's education is also likely to generate negative effect on women's fertility (Shrivastava, 1996; Raj, 1996).

Table 4.15 also shows the relationship between the two variables in the expected direction. For example, among the Hindus, there is a difference of 0.8 children to women whose husbands are more than middle school educated and those husbands who are illiterates. But the difference of children between the two educational levels goes up to 1.6 for the Muslim women. Furthermore, it is seen that the mean number of children living is higher for the Muslim women at all levels of education of their husband.

Husband's occupation

Husband's occupation has often been used in the study of fertility behaviour as an important determinant. Husband's occupation, to a great extent, determines the overall economic condition of the family (Shrivastava, 1996; Raj, 1996).

The mean number of children living has been found to be higher for the Hindu and Muslim women whose husbands' occupation is agriculture/farming. Likewise, the mean number of children living varied for the Hindu and Muslim women according to the other occupations of the husband as well, except for the occupation of service.

Standard of living of the family

Income of the family largely reflects the standard of living of the family. Income and economic conditions of a family do play a role in shaping up the fertility behaviour of a family (Raj, 1996; Shrivastava, 1996). Therefore, it can be expected that as the standard of living of the family goes up, the mean number of children living should decline.

Variation is observed in the mean number of children living for the Hindu women by the standard of living of the family. However, among the Muslim women, the standard of living of the family has significant effect on the mean number of children living. For example, between the two levels of standard of living, namely low and high, the Hindu women have difference of 0.5 children as against the difference of 1.2 children for the Muslim women.

Ever use of family planning methods

It has been found in the present study that the variable 'ever use of family planning methods' has no significant effect on the mean number of children living for the Hindu women.

However, this variable shows significant effect on the mean number of children living to the Hindu and Muslim women as the non-users of family planning methods have higher mean number of children living than the users of the family planning methods. For instance, the Hindu and Muslim women who ever used contraceptives have mean number of children living of 1.9 and 2.5 respectively. But the mean number of children living goes up to 2.3 for the Hindu women and 3.2 for the Muslim women who have never used contraceptives.

Experience of child loss

High fertility is the biological and behavioural response to high mortality (Davis, 1945). This viewpoint is further highlighted in the theory of demographic transition, which says that mortality decline leads to the fertility decline (Davis, 1983). In other words, high mortality rate in a society will keep the fertility rate also on the higher side. Sometimes, however, high mortality may be the result of high fertility in a society also, instead of it being acting as a causative factor of high fertility.

The present study also substantiates the fact that women who had experienced child loss in their past lives have higher fertility than the others (Table 4.15). For instance, the Hindu women who have experienced child loss in the past have the mean number of children living of 2.4 as against the mean number of children living of 2.1 for those who have not experienced child loss. Likewise, the mean number of children living is 3.5 and 2.8 respectively for the Muslim women experiencing child loss and not experiencing child loss.

Exposure to the media

The present study does not show any profound effect of media exposure on the mean number of children living for both Hindu and Muslim women, though the mean number of children living declines for the women with high media exposure as compared to those who have low media exposure.

The mean number of children living of the Hindu and Muslim women comes down from 2.2 to 1.8 for the Hindu women and from 3.2 to 1.8 for the Muslim women when the women are considered by the low and high media exposure.

Determinants of fertility: Results of multiple classification analyses

Attempt has been made in this section to test the first hypothesis of this study that "The various socio-economic factors that determine fertility are different for Hindus and Muslims." This section begins with the efforts to assess the effect of religion on fertility of the Hindu and Muslim women *vis-à-vis* selected background variables.

It is, however, not easy to assess the effect of religion on the mean number of children living. This is because the background socio-economic variables of the women like the education of the woman, occupation of the husband, place of residence, etc. are intricately linked with each other and also with the women's religious beliefs. These factors together, in turn, shape up the various decisions of the couple, including their reproductive decision.

Therefore, to measure the effect of each of the inter-correlated predictor variables chosen for the study upon the dependent variable, i.e. mean number of children living to the women, the statistical technique 'Multiple Classification Analysis' has been used.

After statistically controlling the effect of various socio-economic variables on the dependent variable, the gap of mean number of children living between Hindu and Muslim women may either increase or decrease. If the gap increases, then we can conclude that religion does affect the fertility of the women. On the other hand, after controlling the effect of the background variables, the gap of mean number of children living between the Hindu and Muslim women decreases, then we shall derive the conclusion that religion plays no significant role in determining the fertility of the women. In other words, it will imply that socio-economic factors are far more important factors affecting fertility than religion as such.

Altogether nine background variables, namely place of residence, type of the family in which the women live, women's age at marriage, women's education, women's work status, husband's education, husband's occupation, standard of living of the family, and experience of child loss are chosen and included in the multiple classification analysis model as the control variables for religion to know their impact on fertility. The codes and categories of the above variables are shown in the **Appendix D**. The current age of the women has been entered in the model as the covariate. No interaction term is found significant among the variables chosen for the model and, therefore, no interaction term is entered in the model.

Table 4.16: Multiple classification analyses of the mean number of children living of the Hindu and Muslim women

Religion	*Unadjusted mean*	*Adjusted mean*	*Significance*
Hindu	2.1	2.3	***
Muslim	2.9	2.7	

*** Significant at 1 per cent level

Eta(η) = 0.29; Beta (β) = 0.15 and $R^2 = 0.47$

The result of the analysis has been presented in Table 4.16. The results show that socio-economic factors are more pronounced in affecting fertility than religion. In other words, the results are consistent with the characteristics hypothesis. This is because, before the control of the selected background variables, the fertility differential between the Hindu and Muslim women is that of 0.8 children. However, after the statistical control of the effect of the selected background variables, the fertility differential decreases to 0.4 children.

This is also shown by the correlation ratios of eta (η) and beta (β). Eta and beta are two accompanying statistics (i.e., correlation ratio), which are a by-product of the MCA. Eta indicates the ability of the predictor, using the given categories, to explain variation in the dependent variable without adjusting the other categories. Beta provides a measure of the ability of the predictor to explain variation in the dependent variable after adjusting for the effects of all other predictors (Ladusingh and Bijoy, 2004).

The correlation ratio decreases from 0.29 to 0.15 after the control of the background variables. In other words, the eta value shows religion's 29 per cent ability to explain variation in the mean number of children living when the background variables are not controlled. On the other hand, the beta value shows that the ability of religion to explain the variation in the mean number of children living decreases to 15 per cent when effects of other background variables are controlled.

Therefore, it appears that the difference in the mean number of children living between the Hindu and Muslim women is basically due to the compositional differences in the socio-economic and demographic characteristics of the women and not merely due to the religious differential.

Factors affecting Hindu fertility

ANOVA applied in the preliminary study on the eleven background variables have shown that eight variables have significant bearing on the dependent variable, i.e. mean number of children living of the Hindu women. The eight variables are as follows:

(i) Age at marriage,
(ii) Place of residence,
(iii) Type of family,
(iv) Women's education,
(v) Husband's education,
(vi) Husband's occupation,
(vii) Ever use of contraceptives, and
(viii) Standard of living.

Along with these variables, age of the women has been entered as the covariate in the MCA model, without any interaction term.

Among the eight variables chosen for the model, husband's education and husband's occupation have been found to be the most significant variables affecting the fertility of the Hindu women, before the control of the background variables (Table 4.17). Difference of 1.0 child is observed between the women who are more than middle school educated as compared to the illiterate women and whose husbands are engaged as agriculturists/farmers in comparison to those engaged in the occupation of service. After statistically controlling the effect of other predictor variables on the dependent variable, the difference of mean number of children living between the two categories of the education level of the women and two occupations of the husbands come down to 0.5 children and 0.6 children respectively. Thus, it signifies that even after controlling the effect of other variables, there remains a significant negative effect on the fertility of the Hindu women by husband's education and husband's occupation.

Likewise, age at marriage of the women and standard of living show negative effect on the fertility. After introducing the adjustment for other predictors, the fertility differential by women's age at marriage decreases from 0.6 children to 0.4 children and from 0.5 children to 0.2 children by the standard of living.

It, therefore, means that age at marriage, women's education, husband's occupation and standard of living negatively affect the fertility of the women, even after the control of the background variables.

Table 4.17: Multiple classification analysis of the determinants of fertility (i.e. mean number of children living) of the Hindu women

Background variables	*Mean CEB*		*Significance*
	Unadjusted	*Adjusted*	
Age at marriage			
< 18 Years	2.6	2.4	**
≥ 18 Years	2.0	2.0	
Place of residence			
Rural	2.4	2.2	
Urban	1.9	2.0	
Type of family			
Nuclear	2.0	2.0	
Joint	2.3	2.2	
Women's education			
Illiterate	2.9	2.5	*
Primary	2.3	2.1	
Middle school +	1.9	2.0	
Husband's education			
Illiterate	2.7	1.9	
Primary	2.3	2.2	
Middle school +	1.9	2.0	
Husband's occupation			
Agriculture/Farming	2.8	2.5	**
Service	1.8	1.9	
Business	1.9	2.0	
Others	2.5	2.3	
Ever use of contraceptives			
No	2.3	2.1	
Yes	1.9	2.1	
Standard of living			
Low	2.4	2.2	*
High	1.9	2.0	

$R = 0.62$, $R^2 = 0.39$, $N = 236$

** Significant at 5 per cent level

* Significant at 10 per cent level

Factors affecting Muslim fertility

Table 4.18 provides information about the determinants of fertility of the Muslim women. On the basis of ANOVA in the preliminary study and the significance level, seven variables have been chosen to study the fertility differential of the Muslim women. The seven selected for the purpose are as follows:

(i) Age at marriage of the women,
(ii) Women's education,
(iii) Husband's education,
(iv) Husband's occupation,
(v) Experience of child loss,
(vi) Ever use of contraceptives, and
(vii) Standard of living.

Along with these variables, age of the women has been entered as the covariate in the model. No interaction term is used in the MCA model as no interaction term is found to have statistical significance.

Among the seven variables, 'women's education' has been found to be the most significant variable affecting fertility of the Muslim women, before the adjustment of the background variables. The fertility differential stood at 1.8 children between the two categories of the Muslim women who were illiterates and those who were more than middle school educated. After the adjustment of the other predictor variables, the differential came down to 0.7 children. However, it still remains a significant determinant of fertility of the Muslim women.

The predictor variable 'age at marriage' shows that the unadjusted mean number of children living stands at 3.6 children for the women married before18 years and 2.2 children for the women married after 18 years and, hence, a fertility differential of 1.4 children between the two groups. However, the adjusted mean number of children living figures are 3.3 children and 2.5 children respectively for the women married before 18 years and the women married after 18 years. Hence, the fertility differential comes down to 0.8 children. Therefore, the variable 'age at marriage' also accounts for significant variation in the fertility differential of the Muslim women even after adjusting the effect of the other predictors included in the model.

The standard of living is another background variable having significant effect on the fertility differential of the Muslim women. The unadjusted mean number of children living to the Muslim women having low and high standard of living are 3.4 and 2.2 children and, hence, a fertility differential of 1.2 children. This fertility differential comes down to 0.4 children, once the other background variables chosen are entered in the model.

The results show that the age at marriage, women's education and the standard of living are the determinants of fertility of Muslim women, which are found statistically significant.

Table 4.18: Multiple classification analysis of the determinants of fertility (i.e., mean number of children living) of the Muslim women

Background variables	*Mean CEB*		*Significance*
	Unadjusted	*Adjusted*	
Age at marriage			
< 18 Years	3.6	3.3	***
≥ 18 Years	2.2	2.5	
Women's education			
Illiterate	3.7	3.2	
Primary	2.8	2.9	
Middle school +	1.9	2.5	
Husband's education			
Illiterate	3.6	3.0	
Primary	3.0	3.0	
Middle school +	2.0	2.7	
Husband's occupation			
Agriculturists	4.1	3.4	
Service	1.8	2.7	
Business	2.8	2.9	
Others	3.2	2.8	
Experience of child Loss			
No	2.8	2.9	
Yes	3.5	2.8	
Ever use of contraceptives			
No	3.2	3.0	
Yes	2.5	2.8	
Standard of living			
Low	3.4	3.1	
High	2.2	2.7	

$R = 0.69$, $R^2 = 0.47$, $N = 248$

*** Significant at 1 per cent level

* Significant at 10 per cent level

From the findings of the multiple classification model applied on the Hindu and Muslim women, we can comment that the variables that affect the fertility of the Hindu and Muslim women are more or less the same. Therefore, we will have to refute the hypothesis that the various socio-economic variables that affect the fertility of the Hindu and Muslim women are different. The only observation that we can add here is that the magnitude of effect of these variables on the fertility of Hindu and Muslim women may be different due to the disparities in the socio-economic background of the two groups of women.

Conclusion

The fertility and its related behaviour of the Hindu and Muslim women has shown considerable variation when analysed by the background characteristics of the women. Muslim women have exhibited higher level of fertility than the Hindu women.

However, the multiple classification analyses have shown that the religion bears no direct impact on the mean children living to the women, i.e. fertility of the women. The fertility differential between Hindu and Muslim women is basically due to the differences in the composition of the socio-economic characteristics of the women and the family. In other words, religion's impact on fertility is very much dependent on the socio-economic background characteristics of the women. Furthermore, it has been found out that the factors that affect Hindu and Muslim fertility are more or less the same, though the magnitude of their impact may vary between the Hindu and Muslim women.

5

Maternal Health and Treatment Seeking Behaviour

Maternal health care is considered very crucial for the health of both mother and newborn. For example, Pandey *et al.* (2004) in their study found that the neonatal mortality is lower among children whose mothers received 3 or more ANC check ups as compared to those children born to mothers who either did not receive ANC check up or received less than 3 check ups. The utilization of maternal health care services, however, varies from society to society and within society from individual to individual. It depends on a large number of socio-economic-cultural-demographic-psychological factors, which operate at community and individual levels (Das, 2000).

This chapter tries to provide insights on maternal health care experiences of the Hindu and Muslim women. The data, therefore, mainly relate to the health care experiences of the mother during antenatal, natal and post-natal period. **For the purpose of analyses in the present chapter, those women who gave births during the five years period preceding the survey have only been included.**

Antenatal Care

Antenatal care refers to pregnancy related health care provided by a doctor or a health worker in a medical facility or at home. Antenatal care can have a significant bearing on the successful outcome of a pregnancy. The antenatal care includes the provision of iron folic tablets and TT injections that prevent complications at different stages of the pregnancy. For example, tetanus is said to be a major cause of neonatal mortality in developing countries (Pandey *et al.*, 1998; and Stanfield and Galazka, 1984). Likewise, iron deficiency anaemia among mothers is a major threat to safe motherhood and to health and survival of infant because it contributes to low birth weight, lower resistance to infection and impaired development (Pandey *et al.*, 2004). Antenatal care can reduce maternal morbidity and mortality to a great extent because it also includes advice on correct diet during pregnancy and referral to institutional delivery in case of complications, along with the regular medical care.

Table 5.1: ANCs characteristics of the Hindu and Muslim women

ANC characteristics	*Hindu*	*Muslim*
Per cent having ANCs	86.8 (191)	75.0 (168)
Average number of ANCs	5.5	3.9

Source: Field data.

Table 5.1 gives information about the percentage of Hindu and Muslim having antenatal care during their last pregnancy occurring during five years preceding the survey, as well as the average number of antenatal care. It can be seen that around 87 per cent of the Hindu women have had antenatal check-ups during their last pregnancy. On the other hand, the percentage figure of the Muslim women who have gone for the antenatal checkups stands at 75 per cent.

Ideally, for normal cases antenatal care visits after confirmation of pregnancy should be scheduled at intervals of four weeks thereafter (MacDonald and Pritchard, 1980). However, working women from lower socio-economic groups often find it difficult to attend an antenatal clinic this often because they face a loss of wages whenever they attend. Under these circumstances, a minimum of four antenatal visits is recommended, during the third, sixth, eighth and ninth month of the pregnancy (Park and Park, 1989).

As compared to Hindu women's average 5.5 times visit to the health professionals for ANCs, Muslim women's average number of visits stands at 3.9. So not only the higher percentage of Hindu women have gone for ANCs, but also the Hindu women have, on an average, more number of antenatal check ups than the Muslim women.

Antenatal check ups by background characteristics

Looking at the women who had ANCs during their last pregnancy by selected socio-economic variables (Table 5.2), we find that as the age of the women increases, the chances of her having ANCs decrease. For example, 75.0 per cent of the Hindu women in the age group of 35-49 have gone for the ANCs in comparison to 97.3 per cent of the women in the age group of 15-24. Likewise, 82.5 per cent of the Muslim women of the age group of 15-24 have had ANCs, but the figure for the women of the age group of 35-49 having ANCs is only 60.5 per cent.

It is found that the percentages of women having ANCs decrease with the higher birth order. This is found to be true for both Hindu and Muslim women. For the Hindu and Muslim women having 2 or fewer children, the percentages with ANCs stands at 95.7 per cent and 89.0 per cent respectively compared to 60.7 per cent and 59.4 per cent who have 3 or more children.

Likewise, the urban Hindu and Muslim women go for antenatal check ups more than their rural counterparts. Around 94 per cent of urban Hindu women and 88 per cent of the urban Muslim women have had ANCs as compared to 80 per cent and 65 per cent of rural Hindu and Muslim women respectively.

Education of both women and husband bears significant positive effect on the ANCs. For instance, 94.8 per cent of the Hindu women and 97.7 per cent of the Muslim women with education of more than middle school have gone for the ANCs. Likewise, the Hindu and Muslim women whose husbands are having more than middle school education, the respective percentage of the women going for ANCs stands at 96.1 and 96.4 per cent respectively. For the Hindu and Muslim women who are illiterate as well as whose husbands are illiterate, the percentage of antenatal check ups is very low.

Table 5.2: Percentage distribution of the Hindu and Muslim women having ANCs by selected background variables

Background variables	*Hindu*	*Muslim*
Current age		
15-24	97.3 (36)	82.5 (47)
25-34	88.1 (119)	76.6 (95)
35-49	75.0 (36)	60.5 (26)
Number of living children		
1-2	95.7 (157)	89.0 (105)
3 and above	60.7(34)	59.4 (63)
Place of current residence		
Rural	80.0 (88)	65.1 (82)
Urban	93.6 (103)	87.8 (86)
Education of the women		
Illiterate	52.0 (13)	50.0 (41)
Less than middle school	86.3 (69)	85.7 (84)
More than middle school	94.8 (109)	97.7 (43)
Education of husband		
Illiterate	38.9 (7)	50.0 (36)
Less than middle school	81.2 (56)	82.4 (75)
More than middle school	96.1 (122)	96.4 (53)
Media exposure of the women		
Low	76.9 (40)	66.4 (73)
Medium	86.8 (112)	80.6 (79)
High	100.0 (39)	100.0 (16)
Standard of living		
Low	67.5 (27)	48.9 (45)
High	82.9 (58)	65.7 (23)

Source: Field data.

The degree and magnitude of media exposure also seems to play positive role in ANCs. For instance, amongst the Hindu and the Muslim women having high degree of media exposure, 100 per cent of them have gone for the ANCs. The percentage figure comes down to 76.9 per cent for the Hindu women and to 66.4 per cent for the Muslim women having low media exposure. Likewise, the data have shown that as the standard of living goes up, the coverage of antenatal care also goes up.

Types of antenatal services received

The antenatal check ups can help in the safe outcome of the pregnancy only if the women receive proper and adequate antenatal services during their visits to the health centres. The Table 5.3 shows the percentages of women receiving various antenatal services during their last pregnancy. The percentage of the Hindu women who have had their BP measured stands at 82.7 per cent, blood tested at 81.2 per cent and that of receiving iron folic tablets at 97.4 per cent. Likewise, 94.8 per cent of the Hindu women have reported to have received the TT injections and 77.5 per cent have had their urine tested to find out the level of urine sugar and possible infections. Also 69.1 per cent of the Hindu women have said that their weight was taken during the course of the antenatal check ups.

Table 5.3: Per cent distribution of the Hindu and Muslim women according to the basic antenatal services received during the last pregnancy

*Basic services received**	*Hindu*	*Muslim*
BP measured	82.7 (158)	64.9 (109)
Weight taken	69.1 (132)	49.4 (83)
Urine test	77.5 (148)	54.2 (91)
Blood test for anaemia	81.2 (155)	51.2 (86)
TT injection	94.8 (181)	90.5 (152)
Iron folic tablets	97.4 (186)	79.8 (134)
Others	14.7 (28)	12.5 (21)

* Multiple responses.
Source: Field data.

For the Muslim women, 90.5 per cent received TT injection, 79.8 received iron folic tablets and 64.9 had their BP measured. Likewise, 49.4 per cent, 54.2 per cent and 51.2 per cent of them had their weight measured, urine tested and blood tested respectively during their visits to the health centres for antenatal check ups.

Sources of antenatal check ups

Information on the sources of ANCs presented in Table 5.4 suggests that the percentage of women preferring Government doctor/Government hospital for ANCs is higher amongst the Muslim women (54.2 per cent) than the Hindu women (40.3 per cent). On the other hand, 59.2 per cent of the Hindu women have gone to the private doctor/private hospital for seeking antenatal treatment as compared to the 36.3 per cent of the Muslim women.

Table 5.4: Per cent distribution of the Hindu and Muslim women according to the sources of antenatal check ups

Sources of ANCs	*Hindu*	*Muslim*
Government Hospital/Doctor	40.3 (77)	54.2 (91)
Private Hospital/Doctor	59.2 (113)	36.3(61)
Sub-Centre/Nurse	3.7 (7)	8.9 (15)
Others	1.6 (3)	4.2 (7)

Source: Field data.

Auxiliary Nurse Midwives (ANMs) or nurses/sub-centres provided antenatal services to 3.7 per cent and 8.9 per cent of the Hindu women and Muslim women respectively. The percentage of Hindu women to have gone to others like traditional medical practitioner, quacks, friends, relatives, etc. for the antenatal check ups stands at 1.6 per cent and at 4.2 per cent for the Muslim women.

Main reasons of not having antenatal care

The most important reason cited by both Hindu and Muslim women for not having antenatal check up (ANC) is "Did not feel necessary' (Table 5.5). For example, 55.2 per cent of the Hindu women and 50.0 per cent of the Muslim women have said that they did not feel necessary to have antenatal check ups. The percentage of Hindu and Muslim women saying that they could not afford the expenses of the antenatal check ups and, therefore, did not have the check up is 44.8 per cent and 46.4 per cent respectively.

Health service located too far is cited as a reason for not having ANC by 13.8 per cent of the Hindu women and 16.1 per cent of the Muslim women. According to 10.3 per cent of the Hindu women and 26.8 per cent of the Muslim women, they lacked knowledge about the necessity to have ANC. 'Poor service', 'No time to go' and 'Not permitted to go' are few other reasons cited by the women as the reasons for not having ANCs either due to lack of services or inability to access the services.

Table 5.5: Per cent distribution of the Hindu and Muslim women according to the main reason for not having ANC*

Reasons of lack of ANCs	*Hindu*	*Muslim*
Lack of knowledge	10.3 (3)	26.8 (15)
Did not feel necessary	55.2 (16)	50.0 (28)
Could not afford	44.8 (13)	46.4 (26)
Too far	13.8 (4)	16.1 (9)
Poor service	3.4 (1)	1.8 (1)
No time to go	—	8.9 (5)
Not permitted to go	6.9 (2)	23.2 (13)
Others	—	3.6 (2)

* Multiple responses.
Source: Field data.

Level of self-reported problems during antenatal period

Pregnancy, which is otherwise a beautiful and joyous event for every married women, has become highly hazardous in India (Rajput, 2002). Women in India face many pregnancy related health problems during their antenatal, natal and post-natal period. Some of them do seek medical treatment for remedy, but many others continue to suffer silently due to many reasons.

The surveyed women were asked about some of the common health problems that they faced during their last pregnancy (Table 5.6). Paleness (34.5 per cent), swelling of hands and face (30.5 per cent) and bleeding (10.9 per cent) were most common health problems faced by the Hindu women. Also unnatural discharge (9.5 per cent), blurred vision (8.6 per cent) and convulsion (8.6 per cent) were the other health problems that Hindu women reported to have faced during their last pregnancy.

Paleness (51.8 per cent), swelling of hands and face (26.3 per cent) and bleeding (21.4 per cent) were the main problems Muslim women reported to have faced during their last pregnancy. Unnatural discharge (17.4 per cent), blurred vision

(8.5 per cent) and convulsion (8.5 per cent) were the other problems faced by the Muslim women.

Table 5.6: Per cent distribution of the Hindu and Muslim women according to the self-reported health problems*

Self-reported problems	*Hindu*	*Muslim*
Swelling of hands and face	30.5 (67)	26.3 (59)
Paleness	34.5 (76)	51.8 (116)
Bleeding	10.9 (24)	21.4 (48)
Blurred vision	8.6 (19)	8.5 (20)
Convulsion and fit	8.6 (19)	8.5 (19)
Unnatural discharge	9.5 (21)	17.4 (39)
Others	6.4 (14)	14.7 (33)

* Multiple responses
Source: Field data.

Sources of treatment

Information about Hindu and Muslim women, facing at least one of the above-mentioned health problems, according to the main source of treatment is presented in Table 5.7. Out of those Hindu and Muslim women who suffered from certain health problems during the antenatal period, 76.4 per cent and 49.5 per cent of them respectively sought medical help.

Table 5.7: Per cent distribution of the Hindu and Muslim women reporting problems during antenatal period by the main source of treatment

Sources of treatment	*Hindu*	*Muslim*
Per cent seeking treatment	**76.4 (107)**	**49.5 (91)**
Government Doctor	29.6 (32)	35.2 (32)
Private Doctor	63.9 (69)	51.6 (47)
Nurse	4.6 (5)	5.5 (5)
Others	1.9 (2)	7.7 (2)

Source: Field data.

The Hindu and Muslim women mainly availed the treatments from the doctors, though some of them went to the nurses as well as used other sources for medical advice. Hindu women preferred private doctor to the Government doctor for the treatment of their health problem(s). For instance, 63.9 per cent and 29.6 per cent of the Hindu women went to private doctor and Government doctor respectively for the treatment. Likewise, Muslim women also preferred the Government doctor to the private doctor. For instance, 51.6 per cent of the Muslim women availed the treatment from the private doctor in comparison to 35.2 per cent who went to the Government doctor for the treatment.

Determinants of antenatal check ups: Results of logistic regression analyses

The predictor variables used for this model are the religion, current age of the women, place of residence, type of family, women's education, husband's education and husband's occupation. The categorization and measurement of the predictors variables entered in the model are provided in the **Appendix D**. The response variable used in the model is 'Antenatal check ups' with two categories of 'Had Antenatal check ups' (code = 0) and 'Did not have antenatal check ups" (code = 1). The results of the logistic regression analyses are presented in Table 5.8.

As we can see, religion acts as an important determinant of antenatal check ups only before the control of the background variables. After the adjustment of the background variables, however, religion loses out its significance as a predictor variable of antenatal check ups.

The older women aged 35-49 are less likely to go for antenatal check ups as compared to the younger women in the age group of 15-24. This is found to be true both before and after the control of the background variables.

The results show women's, husband's education and husband's occupation as three important determinants of having antenatal check ups by the women—both before and after the adjustment of the background variables.

After the adjustment of the background variables, it has been seen that women with less than middle school education and more than middle school education are likely to have antenatal check ups 2.8 times and 5.1 times more than the illiterate women respectively.

Table 5.8: Odd ratios of logistic regression analyses of the antenatal check ups of last pregnancy before and after the adjustment of the background variables

Variables	*Before adjustment* Exp (β)	*After adjustment* Exp (β)
Religion (rc: Hindu)		
Muslim	0.6***	1.2
Current age (rc: 15 - 24 years)		
35-34	0.6	0.4**
35-49	0.3***	0.2***
Place of Current Residence (rc: Rural)		
Urban	3.9***	1.7
Type of family (rc: Nuclear)		
Joint	1.0	0.9
Women's Education (rc: Illiterate)		
Less than middle school	6.0***	2.8***
Middle school & above	21.3***	5.1***
Husband's Education (rc: Illiterate)		
Less than middle school	4.9***	2.3**
Middle school & above	27.3***	7.5***
Husband's Occupation (rc: Agriculture)		
Service	37.6***	10.0***
Business	4.6***	2.4*
Others	1.3	1.8

Note: *** Significant at 1 per cent level
** Significant at 5 per cent level
* Significant at 10 per cent level
The remaining variables acted as the control variables for the particular independent variable in question in the model.

Furthermore, after the adjustment of the background variables, the women by their husbands' education, i.e. less than and more than middle school educated are found to have antenatal check ups 2.3 times and 7.5 times more than the women whose husbands are illiterate.

Likewise, when we consider the women by their husbands' occupation, it seen that those women whose husbands' are in the occupations of service and business, the probability of having antenatal check ups increases by 10.0 times and 2.4 times respectively as compared to the women whose husbands' are farmers. The probability of having antenatal check ups was even higher when the occupation of husbands was considered in isolation in the model, i.e. before the adjustment of the background variables.

Natal Care

Like antenatal period, the care of the pregnant women in the natal period is equally important. From the standpoint of child survival and the health of mother, it is necessary for the delivery to take place in medical hospitals/institutions and if not, at least in hygienic conditions at home under the supervision and assistance of a trained medical practitioner.

Place of delivery of the child

The data pertaining to the place of delivery of the last-born children during the 5 years period preceding the survey are shown in Table 5.9. Out of the 220 Hindu women who gave birth during the 5 years period preceding the survey, 33.2 per cent of them delivered their child at home, whereas the remaining 66.8 per cent had institutional deliveries. Again out of the institutional deliveries, 26.4 per cent of the Hindu women had deliveries in the government hospitals/PHCs/sub-centres and the remaining 40.4 per cent had deliveries in the private hospital.

Table 5.9: Per cent distribution of the Hindu and Muslim women according to the place of delivery of the last child

Place of Deiivery	*Hindu*	*Muslim*
Home	33.2 (73)	58.2 (128)
Hospital/PHC/Sub-Centre	26.4 (58)	24.5 (54)
Private Hospital	40.4 (89)	17.3 (38)

Source: Field data.

In comparison, 58.2 per cent of the Muslim women had home deliveries and the remaining 41.8 per cent of the women had institutional deliveries (Figure 5.1). Out of the institutional deliveries again, 24.5 per cent of the births took place in Government hospitals/PHCs/sub-centres and the per cent of the births that took place in the private hospitals was 17.3 per cent.

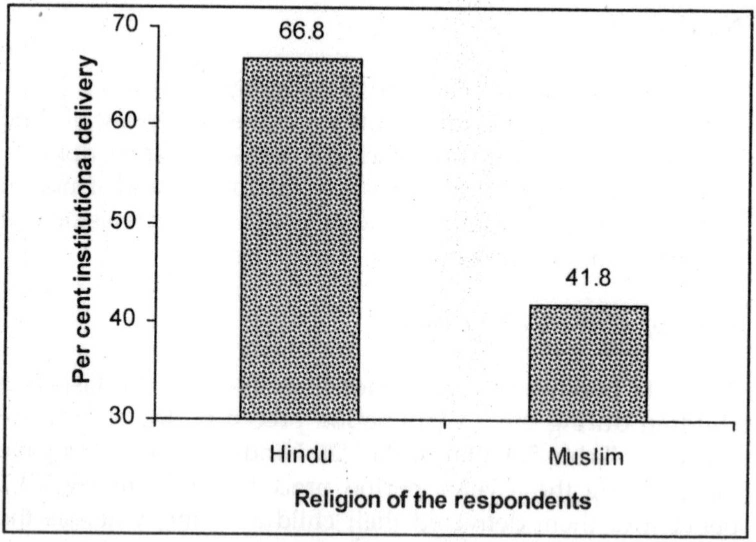

Fig. 5.1: Per cent distribution of Hindu and Muslim women according to the institutional delivery

Institutional delivery of the child by selected background characteristics

Table 5.10 provides data on the institutional delivery of the last-born child of the Hindu and Muslim women by the selected background characteristics. The table suggests that higher the age of the women; lesser is the chance of having institutional delivery of the child, particularly seems to be true for the Hindu women. However, for the Muslim women, the age factor seems to have no influence on the institutional delivery of the child.

When we look at the institutional delivery of the child from the point of view of number of children living, then we notice that the institutional delivery of the child goes down with the higher order birth. In other words, the chance of having institutional delivery is higher for the women going for the first or second child than the higher order birth.

Table 5.10: Per cent distribution of the Hindu and Muslim women having institutional delivery by the background variables

Background variables	*Hindu*	*Muslim*
Current age		
15-24	75.7 (28)	40.0 (22)
25-34	67.4 (91)	42.6 (52)
35-49	58.3 (28)	41.9 (18)
No. of living children		
1-2	79.3 (130)	65.5 (76)
3 and more	30.4 (17)	15.4 (16)
Age at marriage		
Before 18 years	46.8 (22)	18.1 (19)
After 18 years	72.3 (125)	63.5 (73)
Place of current residence		
Rural	50.0 (55)	21.4 (27)
Urban	83.6 (92)	69.1 (65)
Education of the women		
Illiterate	24.0 (6)	10.0 (8)
Less than middle school	66.3 (53)	49.5 (48)
More than middle school	76.5 (88)	83.7 (36)
Education of the husband		
Illiterate	22.2 (4)	10.0 (7)
Less than middle school	60.9 (42)	46.2 (42)
More than middle school	76.4 (97)	75.5 (40)
Standard of living		
Low	50.5 (51)	22.7 (32)
High	80.7 (96)	75.9 (60)

Source: Field data.

Age at marriage is also found to have profound effect on the institutional delivery of the child. For instance, only 46.8 per cent and 18.1 per cent of the Hindu and Muslim women getting married before the age of 18 had institutional delivery of their last child as compared to 72.3 per cent and 63.5 per cent of the Hindu and Muslim women respectively who got married after the age of 18.

The results also show that institutional delivery of the child is higher for the urban women than the rural women. For example, 83.6 per cent and 69.1 per cent of the urban Hindu and Muslim women respectively had their last child deliveries at hospitals in comparison to 50.0 per cent and 21.4 per cent of their rural counterparts.

Educational level of both the women and their husbands are found to be positively related with the institutional delivery of the child, i.e., higher the educational level, higher is the chance that the women will have institutional delivery. This is found to be true for both Hindu and Muslim women.

Last but not the least, standard of living also exerts positive effect on chances of women having institutional delivery of the child. As compared to 80.7 per cent and 75.9 per cent of Hindu and Muslim women with high standard of living, only 50.5 per cent and 22.7 per cent of the Hindu and Muslim women respectively with low standard of living respectively had institutional delivery.

Reasons of non-institutional delivery

According to 39.7 per cent of the Hindu women and 33.6 per cent of the Muslim women, it is their inability to afford the cost of institutional delivery that forces them to have home deliveries of the child (Table 5.11). For 28.8 per cent and 32.0 per cent of Hindu and Muslim women respectively, the decision to have home deliveries of the child is taken by the husbands or in-laws and the women themselves have very little say in that decision.

Table 5.11: Per cent distribution of Hindu and Muslim according to the main reason of non-institutional delivery

Reason	*Hindu*	*Muslim*
Lack of money/Cost too much	39.7 (29)	33.6 (43)
Husband's/In-law's decisions	28.8 (21)	32.0 (41)
Hospital located too far	5.5 (4)	8.6 (11)
Did not feel necessary	20.5 (15)	20.3 (26)
Others	5.5 (4)	5.5 (7)

Around 20 per cent of both Hindu and Muslim women said that they did not go for the institutional delivery of the child because they did not feel necessary for that. The distantly located health centres were the deterrent factor for 5.5 per cent of the Hindu women and 8.6 per cent of the Muslim women in the path of having institutional delivery.

Attendants during home delivery of the child

Data pertaining to home deliveries of the child by the principal person(s) providing assistance are presented in Table 5.12. For those births taking place at home, it is always medically advised to seek the assistance of trained personnel at the time of delivery. However, only 17.8 per cent, 20.5 per cent and 19.2 per cent of the deliveries of the Hindu women were attended by doctor, nurse and trained dai respectively. The corresponding figures for the Muslim women are 7.8 per cent, 11.7 per cent and 21.1 per cent.

Table 5.12: Per cent distribution of the Hindu and Muslim women according to the principal person providing assistance during the home delivery

Attendants	*Hindu*	*Muslim*
Doctor	17.8 (13)	7.8 (10)
Nurse	20.5 (15)	11.7 (15)
Trained *dai*	19.2 (14)	21.1 (27)
Untrained *dai*	15.1 (11)	44.5 (57)
Others	27.4 (20)	14.8 (19)

Source: Field data.

In other words, around 42.5 per cent of the deliveries of the Hindu women and around 59.3 per cent of the deliveries of the Muslim women took place at home without the assistance of properly trained personnel.

Home delivery related care for the mother and the newborn

Various Government agencies have prescribed five minimum cares for deliveries that take place at home. They are maintaining clean surface of the room where the baby is likely to be delivered (including use of properly washed and cleaned bed sheet, etc.), use of clean hands and gloves by the personnel providing assistance during delivery, use of new/clean sterilized blade to cut the umbilical cord, use of clean cord to tie the umbilical cord and leaving the cord stamp clean without the use of any paste or ointment.

Table 5.13: Per cent distribution of the Hindu and Muslim women according to the care taken during the delivery of the last child at home*

Cares	*Hindu*	*Muslim*
Clean surface	92.3	82.7
Clean hands & gloves	80.5	56.8
Clean sterilized blade	88.2	67.3
Clean cord tie	91.8	84.1
Clean cord stamp	75.0	54.5

* Multiple responses.
Source: Field data.

Table 5.13 suggests that the above-mentioned medically prescribed sound and hygienic practices are not followed for many child deliveries taking place at home. This may be either due to the fact that medically trained personnel do not attend many of the deliveries taking place at home or the people are ignorant about those cares.

Level of self-reported health problems during delivery

Institutional delivery of the baby is always advocated because a woman may face many complications at the time of the delivery of the child. Many women even die from the delivery related complications. This happens because of absence of proper medical facilities required for the safe delivery of the baby, particularly for those deliveries that take place at home.

Table 5.14 provides information about the self-reported problems that the married women generally face at the time of delivery. Around 17 per cent and 21 per cent of the Hindu and Muslim women respectively reported to have faced the problem of heavy bleeding which lasted for very long during their last deliveries.

Table 5.14: Per cent distribution of the Hindu and Muslim women reporting different problems during delivery*

Self-reported problems	*Hindu*	*Muslim*
Heavy bleeding which lasted for long	16.8 (37)	21.4 (47)
Retained placenta	8.2 (18)	10.5 (23)
Strong and lasting pain	38.2 (84)	50.9 (112)
Convulsion and fit	2.3 (5)	7.7 (17)

* Multiple responses.
Source: Field data.

Hindu and Muslim women reporting the problem of the placenta remaining inside after the birth were 8.2 per cent and 10.5 per cent respectively. Also 38.2 per cent of the Hindu women had the strong and regular pain during the delivery that lasted long, the corresponding figure for Muslim women is 50.9 per cent. Last but not the least, 2.3 per cent of the Hindu women and 7.7 per cent of the Muslim women experienced convulsion and fit during their last childbirth.

Determinants of institutional delivery: Results of logistic regression analyses

The predictor variables used for this model are the religion, age at marriage of the women, number of children living, place of residence, women's education, husband's education and husband's occupation. The categorization and measurement of the predictor variables entered in the model are provided in the **Appendix D**. The response variable used in the model is 'Institutional delivery' with two categories of 'Did not have institutional delivery' (code = 0) and 'Had institutional delivery' (code = 1).

The results of the logistic regression analyses presented in Table 5.15 show that religion acts as an important determinant of institutional delivery, however, only before the control of the background variables. After the adjustment of the background variables, religion loses out its significance as a predictor variable of institutional delivery, even though Muslim women still show the lower probability of having institutional delivery compared to the Hindu women.

Age at marriage turns out to be a significant variable factor affecting the place of delivery of the child. After the control of the background variables, however, the women marrying after the age of 18 are 1.8 times more likely to go for institutional delivery, compared to the women marrying before the age of 18.

Table 5.15: Odd ratios of logistic regression analyses of place of delivery of last pregnancy before and after the adjustment of the background variables

Variables	*Before adjustment* Exp (β)	*After adjustment* Exp (β)
Religion (rc: Hindu)		
Muslim	0.4***	0.6
Age at marriage (rc: Before 18 years)		
After 18 years	6.0***	1.8*
No. of children living (rc: ≤ 2)		
≥ 2	0.1***	0.2***
Place of Current Residence (rc: Rural)		
Urban	6.3***	4.6***
Women's Education (rc: Illiterate)		
Less than middle school	8.6***	2.7**
Middle school & above	23.7***	1.9
Husband's Education (rc: Illiterate)		
Less than middle school	7.7***	2.3*
Middle school & above	22.3***	3.0**
Husband's Occupation (rc: Agriculture)		
Service	40.9***	18.6***
Business	7.9***	5.1***
Others	2.1	3.3**

Note: *** Significant at 1 per cent level
** Significant at 5 per cent level
* Significant at 10 per cent level
The remaining variables acted as the control variables for the particular independent variable in question in the model.

The results further show that the women having more than 2 children living are less likely to go for institutional delivery in comparison to the women having 2 or less than 2 children. Likewise, the urban women show higher probability of having institutional delivery than the rural women. The urban women are 4.6 times more likely to have institutional delivery than the rural women.

After the adjustment of the background variables, it has been seen that women with less than middle school education are 2.7 more likely to have institutional delivery than the illiterate women.

Furthermore, after the adjustment of the background variables, when the women are considered by their husbands' education, the women whose husbands are less than and more than middle school educated are found to go for institutional delivery 2.3 times and 3.0 times more than the women whose husbands are illiterate.

Husbands' occupation is another important determinant of institutional delivery of the child. The women whose husbands' are in the occupations of service and business, the probability of having institutional delivery increases by 18.6 times and 5.1 times respectively as compared to the women whose husbands' are farmers/agriculturists.

Post-natal Care

Lack of adequate follow up health measures of mothers is another major concern. In fact, many women may face lots of after birth health problems and complications. In the absence of proper follow-up health care measures, these women may be forced to suffer considerably. Sometimes that may even cause serious long-term health complications.

In this section, therefore, effort is made to identify some of the common health problems that mothers face during the post-natal period as well as also their sources of treatment in case of such health problems.

Level of self-reported health problems during post-natal period

Table 5.16 presents the results obtained on self-reported health problems that the surveyed women faced during the first 6 weeks after the delivery.

Pain in abdomen is the major problem that the Hindu women (25 per cent) and paleness that the Muslim women (32.3 per cent) reported. The percentage of Hindu women reporting paleness stands at 18.6 per cent and the percentage of Muslim women reporting the problem of pain in abdomen is 28.6 per cent.

High fever with foul discharge was experienced by 17.3 per cent of the Hindu women and 24.1 per cent of the Muslim women in the immediate post-natal period. Likewise, 5.0 per cent of the Hindu women reported to have faced the problem of excessive bleeding compared to the 11.8 per cent of the Muslim women. Furthermore, 1.8 per cent and 8.6 per cent of the Hindu and Muslim women reported to have experienced convulsion and fit. Besides the above-mentioned problems, 4.5 per cent of the Hindu women and 3.6 of the Muslim women reported some other problems that they faced during the post-natal period.

Table 5.16: Per cent distribution of the Hindu and Muslim women according to different problems experienced during the first 6 weeks after delivery*

Self-reported problems	*Hindu*	*Muslim*
Excessive bleeding	5.0 (11)	11.8 (26)
High fever with foul discharge	17.3 (38)	24.1 (53)
Paleness	18.6 (41)	32.3 (71)
Convulsion/fit	1.8 (4)	8.6 (19)
Pain in abdomen	25.0 (55)	28.6 (63)
Any other	4.5 (10)	3.6 (8)

* Multiple responses.
Source: Field data.

Sources of treatment

For the treatment of the post-natal health problems (Table 5.17), amongst the 57 Hindu women and 76 Muslim women who went for treatment, both Hindu and Muslim women relied mainly on the services of the doctors. For example, 91.2 per cent of the Hindu women and 82.9 per cent of the Muslim women went to the doctors for the treatment.

Again as far as the doctors are concerned, 57.9 per cent of Hindu women went to the private doctors and 33.3 per cent of them went to the Government doctors. On the other hand, 51.3 per cent of the Muslim women went to the private doctors and 31.6 per cent went to the Government doctors for the treatment of the health problems faced during the post-natal period.

Table 5.17: Per cent distribution of the Hindu and Muslim women reporting problems during the post-natal period according to the main source of treatment

Sources of treatment	*Hindu*	*Muslim*
Government doctor	33.3	31.6
Private doctor	57.9	51.3
Nurse	7.0	7.9
Trained *dai*	—	2.6
Others	1.8	6.6
Per cent seeking treatment	**48.3 (57)**	**52.8 (76)**

Source: Field data.

As far as nurses are concerned, 7.0 per cent of the Hindu women and 7.9 per cent of the Muslim women preferred to go to them. Other sources such as the services of traditional medical practitioners like *Hakim, Kabiraj, dai,* etc. and even quacks accounted for 1.8 per cent and 6.6 per cent of post-natal health problems of the Hindu and Muslim women respectively.

Conclusion

The women face various health problems during antenatal, natal and post-natal period, irrespective of their religious affiliation. It can, therefore, be safely said that the various maternal health problems do not vary much across religion, although the magnitude of the problems might vary between the two groups to some extent. However, when the Hindu and Muslim women were cross-analysed by their background characteristics, certain variations were observed between the two groups of the women.

For antenatal check ups, it was seen that the Hindu women preferred the services of the private doctors whereas the Muslim women preferred the Government doctors. Since the Muslim women have lower socio-economic status than the Hindu women, they preferred to go to Government hospitals so as to avail the doctor's services as well as services in respect of TT injection, and iron folic tablets free of cost.

But, for other health problems, the Muslim women preferred to go to private doctors like their Hindu counterparts. However, though both Hindu and Muslim women suffer from various reproductive health problems, the impact of the health problems falls more heavily on the Muslim women as their treatment seeking is lower than the Hindu women.

6

Summary, Conclusions and Future Research Perspectives

This chapter recapitulates the salient features of the book based on the results of the study and conclusions have been drawn and recommendations have been made. The central theme of the study revolves around the efforts to find out the fertility and reproductive health behaviour of the Hindu and Muslim women as well as the effect of selected background variables on their behaviour.

Summary

Statement of the problem

Religion, one of the oldest socio-cultural characteristics associated with the mankind and civilizations created by them over thousands of years of known history, is practiced by almost all societies and it really acts as a powerful system of social control. Many studies have shown that religion has a profound impact on fertility decisions and fertility behaviour of the followers.

India is a country of many religions. Hindus and Muslims are the two major religious communities of India. This is true for Assam too—one of her states located in the North Eastern part of the country. According to the Census of India 2001, the Hindu and Muslim population accounted for 64.89 and 30.92 per cent respectively of the total population of Assam. In fact, according to the 2001 Census, Assam ranks second among all states of India in terms of percentage of Muslim population to total population.

Studies have shown that the Muslims in India exhibit higher level of fertility than the Hindus. Similar pattern is exhibited in Assam too. Why do the religious differences in fertility exist? The 'Characteristics Hypothesis' contends that the fertility differences among different religions are mainly due to the differences in the socio-economic and demographic characteristics of the members of different religious groups.

In recent years, interest has also grown in examining community influences on individual health outcomes, so as to place health care seeking behaviour in its socio-economic context. Studies have shown that the use of reproductive health care services is influenced by individual and household characteristics. Studies of health service use highlight a range of modifying factors in a woman's propensity to seek health care that include demographic, socio-economic and health experience characteristics. However, the various socio-economic and demographic factors are quite often mediated by cultural influences that shape the way an individual perceives his or her own health and the health services available.

Need for the study

Continuous rapid population growth in Assam, to a great extent, has impeded her socio-economic progress over the years. This rapid population growth in Assam is mainly attributed to the high level of fertility. Besides rapid growth of the total population, the religious composition of the population of the state has also undergone change over the years. Differential fertility rates have been cited as the factors responsible for differential growth of population of different religions.

Furthermore, the differential fertility rates of the two religious groups vary across different districts of Assam. So it was considered worth undertaking a district level study to find out the religious differential in fertility in the context of the socio-cultural set up of the Hindu and Muslim population. In the first part of the report, an attempt is made to explain the religious difference in fertility of the Hindu and Muslim women on the backdrop of the 'Characteristics Hypothesis.'

One important aspect of the past fertility reduction policies of the Government was that it failed to take into account the reproductive health needs of the people, particularly that of the married women. However, keeping in view the paradigm shift in the population policy framework that has taken place after the International Conference on Population and Development (1994), held in Cairo, this study has tried to get insights on some of the basic reproductive health behaviour of two major religious communities of Assam in the second part of the report.

Objectives

The specific objectives of the proposed study are:

1. to find out the existing level of fertility and fertility behaviour among Hindus and Muslims.
2. to find out the effect of important socio-economic variables of fertility and fertility behaviour among Hindus and Muslims.
3. to find out the maternal health care experience of these communities of Assam, viz. the maternal health problems, treatment behaviour and avenues of treatment seeking, in case of health problems.
4. to find out the effect of important socio-economic variables on the basic reproductive health behaviour of Hindus and Muslims.

Research hypotheses

Following are the research hypotheses to be investigated in the present study:

1. The various socio-economic factors that determine fertility are different for Hindus and Muslims.

2. The basic reproductive health problems do not vary across Hindus and Muslims.
3. The basic reproductive health behaviour varies among the Hindus and Muslims.

Methodology

The present study mainly tries to examine the differentials in fertility behaviour between the Hindu and Muslim women. Since the attempt is to explain the fertility differential of the Hindu and Muslim women on the basis of the characteristics hypothesis, it is expected that the fertility differential between the two groups would come down after the statistical control of the selected background socio-economic variables in the Multiple Classification Model. Otherwise, the explanation of the fertility differential between the two religious groups would rest with the particularized hypothesis or with some other variables which are not included in the study.

Therefore, to achieve the above objectives, the Hindu-Muslim differential in fertility and related behaviour are examined using the bivariate tables. In order to study the effect of religion on the study variables, such as use of contraceptives, desire for additional children and fertility, multivariate analyses of logistic regression are also used.

Sources of data

This study is primarily based on the primary data collected from Sonitpur district of Assam during the period of April 2006 to July 2006, using a multi-stage random sampling method. Altogether 503 were surveyed using well-structured and pre-tested interview schedule. Out of the 503 women, 245 were being Hindu women and the rest 258 were Muslim women. The married woman in the age group of 13-49 with at least one live birth is considered as the sampling unit for data collection.

Profile of the respondents and the family

The current age of the women, on the basis of different stages of women's reproductive life, were divided into three categories, namely 15-24, 25-34 and 35-49 for the present study. Majority of the respondents belonged to the age group of 25-34. Around 55.0 per cent of the sample Hindu women and half of the Muslim women belong to this group. The percentages of Hindu and Muslim women in the age group of 15-24 are 15.1 per cent and 22.1 per cent respectively. In the age group of 35-49, there are 29.8 per cent and 27.1 per cent of Hindu women and Muslim women respectively.

The age group in which most of the women had their menarche is 10-14 years. As far as the age at marriage is concerned, many women reported to have got married before the attainment of the legal age of marriage. Against around 20 per cent of Hindu women who have got married before the age of 18, half of the Muslim women have got married before the age of 18.

From the marital status point of view, 95.9 per cent of the Hindu women and 94.2 per cent of the Muslim women are currently married. The remaining percentages of Hindu and Muslim are either separated/divorced or widowed.

In the overall sample, 49.8 per cent and 54.7 per cent of the Hindu and Muslim women respectively are from the rural areas. For the remaining 50.2 per cent and 45.3 per cent of the Hindu and Muslim women respectively, the place of current residence is urban.

The data also portray that majority of the Hindu and Muslim women live in the nuclear family. Nearly two-third of the Hindu women, i.e. 65.3 per cent are found to be living in the nuclear family, against the corresponding figure of 74.0 per cent for the Muslim women

In the field of education, there exists a disparity between the Hindu and Muslim women. Comparatively, the Hindu women are found to be better educated than the Muslim women. This is found to be true for the husbands of the Hindu and Muslim women too.

Work status-wise, most of the Hindu and Muslim women are found involved in household activities. Only 13.1 per cent and 6.6 per cent of Hindu and Muslim women respectively are found out to be working outside their home. The distribution of the respondents' husbands according to their occupation also shows marked variation. However, the highest percentages of the husbands of the Hindu women are engaged in the occupation of service (35.6 per cent), whereas it is the occupation of business for the husbands of the Muslim women (57.3 per cent).

The standard of living of the family is divided in two categories, viz. low and high. Higher percentage of Hindu women is found to live in the family having high standard of living, whereas majority of the Muslim women found living in the family having low standard of living.

The data on media exposure show that the women with high degree of media exposure has been low for both Hindu and Muslim women. For instance, only 18.4 per cent of the Hindu women and 6.6 per cent of the Muslim women fall in the group of women having high degree of media exposure, rest have low media exposure.

Fertility and its related behaviour

The results carried out in this chapter show that the Hindu and Muslim women do exhibit variation in fertility behaviour, viz. in areas like the use of contraception, desire for additional children, etc. This is evident from the analyses of various bivariate tables used in the chapter. For instance, though more or less same percentages of the Hindu and Muslim women know about the contraceptives, their knowledge in respect of some of the specific methods varies. Against 93.1 per cent of the Hindu women knowing about the condom, 80.6 per cent of the Muslim women know about it. Likewise, 80.0 per cent of the Hindu women know about Copper-T compared to only 56.2 per cent of the Muslim women.

In the current use of the family planning methods too, it is found out that against around 52.7 per cent of the Hindu women who are currently using contraceptives, the Muslim women's corresponding figure stands at 36.0 per cent only. Comparatively female sterilization is used more than the male sterilization as a method of family planning. This may due to certain myths and misconceptions attached with male sterilization. Many men have the myth that male sterilization may reduce their masculinity. As a result, more often than not the woman is forced to go for the sterilization.

The results of the logistic regression analyses have shown that the variables that affect the contraceptive use of the Hindu and Muslim women are not exactly the same. In case, the same variable found significant for both Hindu and Muslim women, the magnitude of its effect on the contraceptive use has been found out to be different for the Hindu and Muslim women. As far as the religion is concerned, it is found out to be a significant factor affecting the contraceptive use of the women, however, only before the control of the background variables. After the control of the background variables, the significance of religion as an explanatory variable of contraceptive use disappears.

Son preference is prevalent in both Hindu and Muslim societies. Among the Hindu and Muslim women desiring to have additional children, 61.4 per cent of the Hindu women and 53.0 per cent of the Muslim women want their next child to be a male child. The son preference is particularly very high among the aged women. This may be due to the fact that they have already approached the end of their reproductive period and, hence, they are desperate to have a son. The education level of the women has been found to have little bearing on the son preference of the women. The result of logistic regression analysis on desire for additional children shows that Muslim women are more likely to desire for additional children than their rural counterparts.

Breastfeeding is considered very important for the health of the infants and the mother. Breastfeeding improves the nutritional status of young children and reduces morbidity and mortality. There are other beneficial effects for the mother too. Though breastfeeding practice is almost universal amongst the Hindu and Muslim women, only 46.7 per cent of the Hindu women and 36.2 per cent of the Muslim women had breastfed their child within 2 hours of births. The percentages of Hindu and Muslim women breastfeeding without squeezing out the first milk stand at 40.0 per cent and 33.8 per cent respectively.

The background variables of the Hindu and Muslim women are found to exert differential influence on their breastfeeding practices. As far as the religion is concerned, Muslim women are lesser likely to breastfeed their babies without squeezing out the first milk than their Hindu counterparts.

From the point of view of outcome of last pregnancies, 97.3 per cent and 95.1 per cent of the pregnancies of Hindu and Muslim women respectively culminated in live births. The remaining percentages of the pregnancies resulted in stillbirth, induced abortion and spontaneous abortion. Therefore, if safe motherhood is to become a reality, a lot needs to be done in this regard. The occurrences of stillbirth, induced abortion and spontaneous abortion may be due to the lack of awareness among the women about certain precautions and care that they need to take during pregnancy or their inability to take those precautions and afford medical care in case of emergency.

As far as the fertility of the Hindu and Muslim women is concerned, it has been found that the mean number of children living and children ever born are higher for Muslim women than the Hindu women. The mean number of children living and mean number of children ever born for Muslim women are found out to be 2.9 and 3.2 per cent respectively as against the Hindu women's corresponding figures of 2.1 and 2.2 per cent. Likewise, more Hindu women are found to have smaller family size than the Muslim women. In totality, 70.7 per cent of the Hindu women are found to have 2 or less than 2 children, while the corresponding figure for the Muslim women is 48.0 per cent.

The fertility of the Hindu and Muslim women has shown considerable variation when analysed by the background characteristics of the women. However, the multiple classification analyses have shown that the religion bears no direct impact on the mean number of children living to the women, i.e. fertility of the women. The fertility differential between Hindu and Muslim women is basically due to the differences in the composition of the socio-economic characteristics of the women and the family. In other words, religion's impact on fertility is very much dependent on the socio-economic background characteristics of the women. Furthermore, it has been found out that the factors that affect Hindu and Muslim fertility are more or less the same.

Maternal health and its related behaviour

Maternal health care is considered very crucial for the health of both mother and newborn. The care during antenatal, delivery and the post-natal period determines the health of the mother and the child. The availability of the services and their utilization is, therefore, very important for the mother's and child health. However, the utilization of those services varies from society to society and within society from group to group and within group from individual to individual. It mainly depends on the large number of socio-economic-cultural factors which operate at the individual and community level.

In this chapter, efforts were made to identify the health problems that the married women generally face during the antenatal, natal and post-natal period, and the utilization of the health services during the maternal period. The health problems and the utilization of the health services were also examined by selected set of background variables. Logistic regression analyses were used to find out the determinants of some of the health behaviours, such as the utilization of the antenatal services, place of delivery, etc. For the purpose of policy significance, however, those women who gave birth to a child during the five-year period preceding the survey were only included in the study.

Around 13 per cent of the Hindu women and 25 per cent of the Muslim women did not have antenatal check ups during their last pregnancy. The average number of antenatal check ups for the Hindu women and Muslim women stands at 5.5 times and 3.9 times respectively. As far as the background variables are concerned, current age of the women and the number of children living are inversely related with the antenatal check ups, whereas the place of residence, education of the women, education of the husband, media exposure and standard of living are positively related with the antenatal check ups.

The main reasons cited by the Hindu and Muslim women for non-utilisation of the antenatal services are 'did not feel necessary'. This may be due to their traditional belief that childbirth is the gift of God and, hence, they do not require any medical intervention. Inability to afford the expenses also comes in the way of availing antenatal services. Some other reasons mentioned were 'lack of knowledge of ANCs' and 'health institutions are located too far'. Even those Hindu and Muslim women had ANCs, according to them, the services that they received were not complete and up to the mark. For instance, many women, particularly the Muslim women did not have urine test for infection, blood test for anaemia, did not receive iron folic tablets, etc. during the ANCs.

The results of logistic regression analysis show that the most significant background variables of the women that affect the utilization of the antenatal services are the current age of the women, women's education, husband's education and husband's occupation. The results also show that the self-reported health problems of the women do not vary much between the Hindu and Muslim women. However, in case of the sources of treatment, it is found that the Hindu women generally prefer the services of the private doctors whereas the Government doctors are the preferred source of treatment for the Muslim women.

The data pertaining to the place of delivery of the last-born children during the five-year period preceding the survey show that many deliveries of the child took place at home. The percentage of home deliveries is found to be higher for the Musiim women than the Hindu women. Around 33 per cent and around 58 per cent of the deliveries of the children of the Hindu and Muslim women respectively took place at home. As far as the reasons of non-institutional delivery are considered, around 40 per cent and 34 per cent of the Hindu and Muslim women respectively cited 'lack of money' as the main factor, followed by 'decisions of husbands/in-laws' and 'did not feel necessary'. The Hindu women citing the preceding two reasons stand at 29 per cent and 21 per cent respectively. The percentages of Muslim women stating the above two reasons are 32 per cent and 20 per cent respectively.

The data also point to the fact that trained medical or para-medical persons do not attend many of the births taking place at home. For example, doctors and nurses attended only 17.8 per cent and 20.5 per cent of the deliveries of the Hindu women respectively and 7.8 per cent and 11.7 per cent of the deliveries of the Muslim women respectively. Moreover, many home deliveries of the children took place under unhygienic conditions as the basic cares that the attendant needed to take during delivery were compromised with. This may be due to the fact that medically trained personnel do not attend many of the deliveries taking place at home.

Many women suffer from various health problems during the post-natal period also due to the lack of proper and adequate follow up measures. For instance, 25.0 per cent of the Hindu women reported the problem of pain in abdomen and 32.3 per cent of the Muslim women cited paleness as the main problem that they faced during the post-delivery period (up to six weeks).

The findings of this chapter substantiate the hypothesis that various maternal health problems do not vary much across religion. In other words, irrespective of the religious background, women were found to have suffered from various health problems during pre-delivery, delivery and post-delivery period, though the magnitude of the problems might vary between the two groups to some extent. However, when the Hindu and Muslim women were cross-analysed by their background characteristics, certain variations were observed between the two groups of the women.

As far as the hypothesis of differential behaviour is concerned, a specific behaviour was not observed. For antenatal check ups, it was seen that the Hindu women preferred the services of the private doctors whereas the Muslim women preferred the Government doctors. Since the Muslim women have lower socio-economic status than the Hindu women, they preferred to go to Government hospitals so as to avail the doctor's services as well as services in respect of TT injection, and iron folic tablets free of cost.

But, for other health problems, the Muslim women preferred to go to private doctors like their Hindu counterparts. However, though both Hindu and Muslim women suffer from various reproductive health problems, the impact of the health problems falls more heavily on the Muslim women as their treatment seeking is lower than the Hindu women.

Conclusions and Suggestions

The background profile of the women and their families shows that the Muslim women and their husbands are educationally disadvantaged than their Hindu counterparts. That was also reflected in the data on the husbands' occupation. The percentage of the husbands of the Muslim women working in the occupation of service was very low. Likewise, comparatively Muslim families are found to have lower standard of living than the Hindu families.

The knowledge of family planning method is quite evenly spread amongst the Hindu and Muslim women. However, the use is not that widespread, and Hindu-Muslim differential in the current use of contraception is observed. The current use of contraception has been found out to be very low for the Muslim women.

Given the fact that around 41per cent of the Hindu women and 45 per cent of the Muslim women desire additional children, the need to increase the contraceptive use cannot be exaggerated. Emphasis, therefore, should be placed on the introduction of an effective Information, Education and Communication (IEC) programme to raise awareness on contraceptive use. Male's involvement in the use of the contraceptive must also be encouraged. Furthermore, easy availability of the contraceptives has to be ensured so that the couples can easily access them if they so desire.

The study shows that the son preference is quite high among the Muslim women as well. Traditionally it has been projected that Hindus only have very high degree of son preference. The son preference is also found to be very high among the aged women. With the increase in the age, women's desperation to have a son also rises. This is found true for both Hindu and Muslim women.

Though breastfeeding is almost universal, many Hindu and Muslim women are ignorant about the beneficial effects of the first milk of mother which contains colostrum. Generation of awareness amongst the women in this regard can benefit both the mothers and child immensely.

Though the Muslim women exhibit higher level of fertility than the Hindus, the statistical analyses have ruled out the significant role of religion as an explanatory variable in the higher level of fertility of the Muslim women. Likewise, in other related areas of fertility like use of contraception, desire for additional children, etc., the influence of religion has not been well substantiated. As the multiple classification analyses suggest, the variation in the fertility level of the Hindu and Muslim women can be attributed to the differences in the socio-economic status of the women and the family and not religion as such.

Therefore, any attempt to bring down the Muslim fertility in future must take into account the compositional differences in the socio-economic background characteristics of the women and the family. So there is every need to enhance the education level in the Muslim society, particularly that of the women. Better education coupled with fair access to job opportunities can address the problem of economic backwardness of large section of the Muslim society which can help to bring down the fertility level in the long run.

Since improving the socio-economic status of the Muslims at par with the other sections of the society may take a long time period, an effective Information, Education and Communication (IEC) programme should be implemented vigorously on sustained basis as a short-term measure, along with improving the health delivery system in the Muslim inhabited areas.

However, any attempt to introduce and implement an IEC programme and encourage female education in the Muslim society must take into account the socio-religious constraints, such as the influence of religious clerics that sometimes act as a hurdle in the said process. Involvement of the progressive minded prominent and powerful Muslim leaders and even the clerics of different localities in the said drive can be considered. This can make a huge difference in the successful outcome of any future fertility reduction programme.

The utilization of the antenatal care services has not been found satisfactory. Even those who go for antenatal services, they perceive them as inadequate. Therefore, along with improving the coverage of the antenatal services, improving the quality of the services is very essential.

One of the important factors responsible for low antenatal coverage is due to the fact that most of the doctors practicing in the rural areas are male. This often comes in the way of proper and adequate medical examination of the pregnant women by the doctors. Therefore, to increase the antenatal coverage, along with improving the health care infrastructures with female doctors in every hospital, the need is to educate the women and their families about the significance and benefits of the antenatal care for the mother and child.

Many deliveries take place at home under unhygienic conditions without having the assistance of trained medical personnel. Since institutional delivery of each and every child is not practically possible and feasible, more and more villages must be brought under the intensive care of the ANMs. Likewise, the number of properly trained *dais* should be increased in the rural areas so that they can attend more and more births and provide the medically advised services, at least to those deliveries which do not show any delivery related complications.

Future Research Perspectives

The effect of religion on fertility very much depends on the one's belief and commitment to the doctrines that the religion preaches. Therefore, the fertility behaviour and for that matter any other behaviour of the women will be governed by religion only if she strongly adheres to the religious preaching. However, the data collected for the present study do not furnish any information on such aspect of religion. This aspect of religious behaviour of the women may be taken into account in future research studies.

It is also felt now the need of the use of qualitative methods of data collection to complement the method used in the present study. Therefore, in any future research study of this kind to explore the fertility and reproductive health behaviour of the women, appropriate qualitative methods such as group discussion, key informants, free listing, etc. must appropriately be used.

This study has shown that the age at marriage is lower for the Muslim women. This aspect can be explored in greater length in future studies. Likewise, very high degree of son preference is observed amongst the Muslim women too. This can be an interesting study option. Some other areas that can be explored in future studies are differential contraceptive behaviour, problems of institutional delivery, etc.

Last but not the least, a comparative analysis of Hindu-Muslim differential in fertility on the basis of data collected from a Hindu dominated district, a Muslim dominated district and a district with proportionate Hindu-Muslim population can form the base of an interesting research study.

APPENDIX-A

Interview Schedule

(Confidential—For Research Purpose Only)

Identification

Name of the Respondent : ____________
Name of the Head of the Household : ____________
Name of the Village/Town : ____________

Section-I: Household Information

1.	Religion	Hindu (1)/Muslim (2)
2.	Place of Current Residence	Rural (1)/Urban (2)
3.	Type of Family	Nuclear (1)/Joint (2)
4.	Type of house	Pucca ____ 1 Semi-Pucca ____ 2 Kuccha ____ 3
5.	Separate Room for Cooking	Yes ____ 1 No ____ 2
6.	Source of Lighting	Electricity or Rechargeable Battery or Gas ____ 1 Kerosene or Others ____ 2
7.	Fuel for Cooking	Electricity or Gas or Biogas ____ 1 Coal or Kerosene ____ 2 Firewood or Cow dung or Others ____ 3
8.	Source of Drinking Water	Hand Pump at Home ____ 1 Well at Home ____ 2 Nothing ____ 3
9.	Toilet Facility	Has Toilet ____ 1 No Toilet ____ 2
10.	Ownership of Agro Land	More than 4 Acres ____ 1 1-3 Acres ____ 2 No Land ____ 3

11. Ownership of livestock	Bullock/Buffalo ______ 1 Cow ______ 2 Goat/Sheep ______ 3 Hen/Cock/Duck ______ 4
12. Ownership of Goods	Fan ______ 1 Bicycle ______ 2 T.V. ______ 3 Refrigerator ______ 4 Motorcycle ______ 5 Car ______ 6

Section-II: Respondent's Background

1.	What is your current age? *(Age in completed years)*	[ ]
2.	What is your current marital Status?	Currently Married ______ 1 Married but separated ______ 2 Divorced ______ 3 Widowed ______ 4
3.	What was your childhood residence?	Rural ______ 1 Urban ______ 2
4.	What was your age at menarche? *(Age in completed years)*	[ ]
5.	How old were you at the time of marriage? *(Age in completed years)*	[ ]
6.	What is the highest grade of education you have completed?	Illiterate ______ 1 Primary ______ 2 Middle School ______ 3 Less than secondary passed ______ 4 Secondary passed and above ______ 5
7.	Are you currently working in income earning activities other than household & family work?	No ______ 1 Yes ______ 2
8.	What is the highest grade of education your husband has completed?	Illiterate ______ 1 Primary ______ 2 Middle School ______ 3 Less than secondary passed ______ 4 Secondary passed and above ______ 5

9. What is your husband's occupation?	Farming/Agriculture on own land ______ 1 Service in (Govt)/Organized Private Sector ______ 2 Business ______ 3 Others ______ 4
10. How frequently do you read newspaper?	Everyday ______ 1 Sometimes ______ 2 Never ______ 3
11. How frequently do you watch T.V.?	Everyday ______ 1 Sometimes ______ 2 Never ______ 3
12. How frequently do you listen to radio?	Everyday ______ 1 Sometimes ______ 2 Never ______ 3

Section-III: Fertility and Fertility Related Behaviour

Que	Questions and Filters	Coding Categories	Skip To
1.	How many living sons and daughters do you have including those presently not living with you? *(Include only those surviving children to whom the respondent has given birth)*	Son ______ [ ] Daughter ______ [ ] Total ______ [ ]	
2.	Did any of your children die?	Yes ______ 1 No ______ 2	Q.No.4
3.	If yes, how many sons and daughters?	Son ______ [ ] Daughter ______ [ ] Total ______ [ ]	
4.	Did any of your pregnancy end in abortion or stillbirth?	Yes ______ 1 No ______ 2	Q.No.6
5.	If yes, how many of them were abortion or stillbirth?	Ind. abortion ___ [ ] Sp. abortion ___ [ ] Total stillbirth ___ [ ]	
6.	Do you like to have another child?	Yes ______ 1 No ______ 2	Q.No.8

7.	If yes, would you like to have a son or daughter?	Son ____________1 Daughter __________2 No preference ______3	
8.	What family planning methods are available in your community?	Yes No Female Sterilisation........ (1) (2) Male Sterilisation(1) (2) Copper-T/Loop... (1) (2) Condom (e.g.,Nirodh).......(1) (2) Oral Pill............. (1) (2) Periodic Abstinence......... (1) (2) Withdrawal......... (1) (2) Others............... (1) (2)	
9.	Did you ever use any contraceptive in the past?	Yes ____________1 No______________2	
10.	Are you currently pregnant?	Yes 1 No 2	Sect.-IV
11.	Are you and your husband currently using any family planning method?	Yes ____________1 No ____________2	
12.	Which method you/your husband is currently using?	Female Sterilisation __1 Male Sterilisation ____2 Copper-T/Loop _____3 Condom (Ex.Nirodh) _4 Oral Pill __________5 Periodic Abstinence __6 Withdrawal _______7 Others __________8	
13.	What is the main reason for not using any method?	Hard to get________1 Health problem _____2 Costs too much _____3 Against religion _____4 Not having sex ______5 Infrequent sex ______6 Husband away/ separated _________7 Postpartum/Breast-feeding __________8 Afraid of sterilization__9 Want children______10	

Section-IV: Antenatal, natal and post-natal care

Que	*Questions & filters*	*Coding categories*	*Skip to*
1.	Did you get pregnant during the last 5 years?	Yes ____ 1 No ____ 2	 Sect.-V
2.	If yes, what was the outcome of that pregnancy?	Live birth ____ 1 Still birth ____ 2 Induced abortion ____ 3 Spontaneous abortion _4	
3.	If live birth, what was the sex of the child?	Male ____ 1 Female ____ 2	
4.	Did you go for antenatal check up during the last pregnancy?	Yes ____ 1 No ____ 2	 Q.No.6
5.	If yes, where did you go? *(CIRCLE ALL RESPONSES MENTIONED)*	1. Govt. hospital/ CHC/PHC ____ A 2. Sub-centre ____ B 3. Private doctor/ Pr. hospital ____ C 4. Others ____ D (Specify)	
6.	If yes, how many times? *(Actual number)*	[ ]	
7.	During your visit, did you receive any of the following?	Yes No BP measured ___(1) (2) Weight taken ___(1) (2) Urine test ___(1) (2) Test for anaemia _(1) (2) TT injection ___(1) (2) Iron folic tablets _(1) (2) Others ___(1) (2)	
8.	Why did you not go for antenatal check up? *(CIRCLE ALL RESPONSES MENTIONED)*	1. Lack of knowledge of services ____ A 2. Did not feel necessary ____ B 3. Could not afford ___ C 4. Too far ____ D 5. Poor quality service _E 6. No time to go ____ G 7. Not permitted to go _H 8. Others ____ I (Specify)	

9.	During your last pregnancy, did you suffer from any of the following? *(CIRCLE ALL RESPONSES MENTIONED)*	1. Swelling of hands & face ________A 2. Paleness ________B 3. Bleeding ________C 4. Blurred vision ______D 5. Convulsion/fit ______E 6. Unnatural discharge________F 7. Others__________G (Specify)	
10.	If any, did you consult doctor or health worker for your health problems?	Yes____________1 No ____________2	Q.No. 10
11.	If yes, whom did you consult? *(CIRCLE ALL RESPONSES MENTIONED)*	1. Govt. Doctor_______A 2. Private Doctor______B 3. Govt. Nurse/ANM__C 4. Trained Dai_______D 5. Untrained Dai _____E 6. Others _________G (Specify)	
12.	Where was the baby delivered?	Home ____________1 Govt. Hospital/CHC/ PHC ____________2 Private Hospital_______3 Others____________4 (Specify)	
13.	If delivered at home, who was the principal person to provide assistance?	Doctor____________1 Govt. Nurse/ANM ____2 Trained Dai ________3 Untrained Dai ______4 Friends/Relatives ____5 Others____________6 (Specify)	
14.	Were the following taken care of during delivery? *(CIRCLE ALL RESPONSES MENTIONED)*	1. Clean surface ______A 2. Clean hand & glove_B 3. Clean/sterilized blade __________C 4. Clean cord tie ______D 5. Clean cord stamp __E	
15.	Did you suffer from the following at the time of delivery? *(CIRCLE ALL RESPONSES MENTIONED)*	1. Heavy bleeding which lasted long ________A 2. Retained placenta __B 3. Strong & regular painlasted long ____C 4. Convulsion & fit ____D	

16.	If home, what was the principal reason of not having institutional delivery?	1. Lack of money/Cost too much ______ A 2. Husband/in-laws' decision ______ B 3. Hospitals located quite far ______ C 4. Did not feel necessary ______ D 5. Others ______ F (Specify)	
17.	Did you breastfeed your child?	Yes ______ 1 No ______ 2	Q.No. 15
18.	How soon after the birth did you start breastfeeding? *(Those who had normal birth)*	Same day within 2 hours of birth ______ 1 Same day after 2 hours of birth ______ 2 Afterwards ______ 3	
19.	When you first breastfed your child, did you squeeze out the milk before feeding the child?	Yes ______ 1 No ______ 2	
20.	During the first 6 weeks after the delivery, did you face any of the following problems? *(CIRCLE ALL RESPONSES MENTIONED)*	1. Excessive Bleeding_A 2. High fever with foul discharge ______ B 3. Paleness ______ C 4. Convulsion/fit ______ D 5. Pain in abdomen __E 6. Others ______ F (Specify)	
21.	Did you see any one for the treatment?	Yes ______ 1 No ______ 2	Sect.-V
22.	If yes, whom did you see? *(CIRCLE ALL RESPONSES MENTIONED)*	1. Govt. Doctor ______ A 2. Private Doctor ______ B 3. Govt. Nurse ______ C 4. Trained Dai ______ D 5. Untrained Dai ______ E 6. Others ______ G (Specify)	

APPENDIX-B

Theoretical Background of LR and MCA

Logistic Regression

This technique is used when the response variable is dichotomous (i.e., binary). The predictor variable may be quantitative or categorical or mixture of the two (Clark and Hosking, 1986; Retherford and Choe, 1993).

Thus, the outcome of an event reduces to occurring or not occurring. Here comes the concept of probability. If the event occurs, then the probability (p) is 1, otherwise 0.

In the logit function, the probability of occurring an event is—

$$P = \frac{1}{1+e^{-Z}} = \frac{e^{Z}}{1+e^{Z}} = \frac{\exp(Z)}{1+\exp(Z)}$$

When Z is a linear function of a set of independent variables it becomes a multivariate logistic function, instead of a bivariate function. Thus,

$$Z = b_0 + b_1X_1 + b_2X_2 + \text{———} + b_kX_k.$$

In other words, the probability of not occurring of an event is

$$1 - P = 1 = \frac{1}{1+e^{-Z}} = \frac{e^{-Z}}{1+e^{-Z}}$$

Thus, the odds of occurring an event becomes

$$\frac{P}{1-P} = e^{Z}$$

Clearly P/1–P equals the odds of occurring the event. The logistic model for log odds of given predictor variable is

$$\text{logit P} = \log \frac{P}{1-P} = \text{log odds}$$

It is, however, easier and more convenient to interpret the results in terms of odds ratio instead of log odds. Odds ratio is defined as the ratio of odds of an event when there is an increase of one unit in independent variable holding other variables constant. However, the choice of either log odds or odds ratio is a matter of convenience. When the model is in additive form then log odds is used but when the model is of multiplicative form, then odds ratio is used. In other words, when we consider the log odds as the response variable, the logit model is and additive model, but when we consider the odds as the response variable, the logit model is a multiplicative model (Retherford and Choe, 1993).

Multiplicative Classification Analysis (MCA)

MCA is a technique for examining the relationship between several predictor variables and a dependent variable within the context of an additive model. It is most easily explained as multiple regression with dummy variables (Andrews *et al.*, 1973; Retherford and Choe, 1993). In basic MCA, the response variable is a quantitative variable, and the predictor variables are categorical variables.

The chief advantage of MCA over conventional dummy variables regression is a more convenient arrangement and understandable output that focuses on sets of predictors and the extent and direction of the adjustments made for inter-correlations among the set of predictors. A key feature of the MCA technique is its ability to show the effect of each predictor on the dependent variable both before and after taking into account the effect of all other variables. Another key feature is its freedom from the linearity restriction. The predictors are always treated as sets of classes or categories, so it does not matter whether a particular set represents nominal scale, an ordinal scale or an interval scale. Since the categories of a nominal scale can be placed in any order, one cannot speak of the direction or sign of the relation with the dependent variable or even of the form of its relation to other scales. The MCA coefficients are all expressed as adjustments to the grand mean, not deviations from the single class which must be excluded from each set when dummy variables are used (Ladusingh and Bijoy, 2004).

APPENDIX C

Scores for the Variables used in the Computation of Standard of Living Index (SLI)

Variable	*Scores*
Type of House	Kucha = 0 Semi Pucca = 1 Pucca = 2
Separate Room for Cooking	No = 0 Yes = 1
Source of Lighting	Kerosene or Others = 0 Electricity or Rechargeable Battery or Gas = 1
Fuel for Cooking	Firewood or Cow Dung or Others = 0 Coal or Kerosene = 1 Electricity or Gas or Biogas = 2
Source of Drinking Water	Nothing = 0 Well at Home = 1 Hand Pump at Home/Water Supply at Home = 2
Toilet Facility	No Toilet = 0 Has Toilet = 1
Ownership of Agro land	No Land = 0 1-3 Acres = 1-4 Acres and Above = 2
Ownership of Goods	Fan = 2, T.V. = 2, Refrigerator = 3,Motorcycle = 3, Car = 4
SLI	Score Range = 0 to 25
Categories of SLI	Range—Low = 0-10 High = 11-25

Categorization & Measurement of the Independent Variables of Various Models

Independent variables	*Categorisation & Measurement*
Current age of the women	15-24 25-34 35-49
Age at menarche	Below 10 years, 11-14 years, After 14 years
Age at marriage of the women	Before 18 years, After 18 years
Place of Childhood residence	Rural/Urban
Place of current residence	Rural/Urban
Type of family	Nuclear/Joint
Women's education	Illiterate, Less than middle school, Middle school & above
Women's work status	Not working, Working
Husband's education	Illiterate, Less than middle school, Middle school & above
Husband's occupation	Agriculture, Service, Business, Others
Number of surviving children	Less than and equal to 2 children, More than 2 children
Experience of child loss	No/Yes
Ever use of contraceptives	No/Yes
Standard of living index	Low/Medium/High
Media exposure of the women	Low/Medium/High

Bibliography

Addai, Isaac. 1998. Demographic and socio-cultural factors influencing use of maternal health service in Ghana. *African Journal of Reproductive Health* 2(1): 73-80.

Alagarajan, M. and P.M Kulkarni.1998. Fertility Differentials by Religion in Kerela: A Period Parity Progression Ratio Analysis. *Demography India* 27(1): 213-227.

Andrew, F.M., J.N. Morgan, J.A. Sonquist and L. Klem. 1973. *Multiple Classification Analysis—A Report on a Computer Programme for Multiple Regression using Categorical Predictors*, Michigan: Institute for Social Research, University of Michigan.

Ashraf, A. 1994. *Women's Development in Family Welfare Programme Performance.* Family Planning Association of India: 2-6.

Balsubramanian, K. 1984. Hindu-Muslim Differentials in Fertility and Population Growth in India: Role of Proximate Variables. *Artha Vijnana* 26(3).

Bang, R.A. and A. Bang. 1991. Why women hide them: Rural women's view points on reproductive tract infections. *Manushi* 69: 7-30.

Barrera, A. 1990. The role of maternal schooling and its interaction with public health programmes in child health production. *Journal of Development Economics* 32:69-91.

Basu, Alaka Malwade. 1990. Cultural influences on health care use: Two regional groups in India. *Studies in Family Planning* 21(5): 75-286.

———1997. The Politicisation of Fertility to Achieve Non-Demographic Objectives. *Population Studies* 51: 5-18.

———2000. Gender in Population Research: Confusing implications for health policy. *Population Studies* 54 (1).

Becker, G.S., 1991. *Treaties on the Family*. 2nd Edition, Harvard University Press, Cambridge.

Becker, Marshall H., Lois A. Maiman, John P. Kirscht, Don P. Haefner, and Robert H. Drachman. 1977. The Health Belief Model and prediction of dietary compliance: A field experiment. *Journal of Health and Social Behaviour* 18(4): 348-366.

Bhagat, R.B. and P. Praharaj. 2005. Hindu-Muslim Fertility Differentials. *Economic and Political Weekly* XL (5): 411-418.

Bhat, P.N. Mari and A.J.F. Zavier. 2005. Role of Religion in Fertility Decline: The Case of Indian Muslims. *Economic and Political Weekly* XL (5): 385-402.

Bhatia, Jagdish and John Cleland.1995a. Determinants of maternal care in a region of South India. *Health Transition Review* 5: 127-142.

———1995b. Self-reported symptoms of gynaecological morbidity and their treatment in South India. *Studies in Family Planning* 26(4): 203-216.

Bloom, Shelah S., Theo Lippeveld and David Wypiz.1999. Does antenatal care make a difference to safe delivery? A Study in Urban Uttar Pradesh, India. *Health Policy and Planning* 14 (1): 38-48.

Bongaarts, John. 1978. A Framework for Analyzing the Proximate Determinants of Fertility. *Population and Development Review* 4(1):105-132.

Bongaarts, J. and R. Potter. 1983. *Proximate Determinants of Fertility*. New York: Academic Press.

Borooah, V.K. and S. Iyer. 2005. Religion, Literacy, and the Female to Male Ratio. *Economic and Political Weekly* XL (5): 419-427.

Bose, Ashish. 1969. Differential Fertility by Religion in India, In: A.R. Kamat (ed.), *Population Problems of India*, Monograph, Series No.II, CFPI, New Delhi, 78-83.

———2005. Beyond Hindu-Muslim Growth Rates: Understanding Socio-Economic Reality. *Economic and Political Weekly* XL (5): 370-374.

Cairo Conference. 1994. *International Conference on Population and Development (ICPD)*, September 5-13, United Nations.

Caldwell, John. 1979. Education as factor in mortality decline: An examination of Nigerian data. *Population Studies* 33: 395-413.

———1986. Routes to low mortality in poor countries. *Population and Development Review* 12: 171-220.

———1990. Cultural and social factors influencing mortality in developing countries. *The Annals of the American Academy of Political and Social Science* 510: 44-59.

Caldwell, J. and P. Caldwell. 1988. *Women's position and child mortality and morbidity in LDCs.* Research paper. Canberra: Department of Demography, Research School of Social Sciences, Australian National University.

Caldwell, J.C., P.H. Reddy and Pat Caldwell.1988. *The Causes of Demographic Change: Empirical Research in South Asia.* The University of Wisconsin Press Ltd., Wisconsin.

Cassen, R.H. 1978. *India: Population, Economy, Society.* The MacMillan Company of India Ltd., New Delhi.

Census of India, 1951. Vol - XII, Part II-A, General Population Tables, Office of the Registrar General, India, New Delhi.

———1971. Series-3-Assam, Part-II-C (i), Table-C-VII and C-VIII, Office of the Registrar General, India, New Delhi.

———2001. Data on Religion. Census Data Product No. 00-104-2001-Cen-CD, Office of the Registrar General, India, New Delhi.

Chacko, Elizabeth. 2001. Women's use of contraception in rural India: A village-level study. *Health and Place* 7(3): 197-208.

Chamie, J. 1977. Religious Differentials in Fertility: Lebanon 1971. *Population Studies* 31(2): 365-382.

Chatterjee, M. 1996. Addressing Gender and Poverty Concerns in a Reproductive Health Programme. In: Anthony R. Measham and A. Richard Heaver (eds), *Supplement to India's Family Welfare Programme: Moving to a Reproductive and Child Health Approach,* The World Bank, Washington, pp. 30-45.

Chaudhury, R.H. 1982. *Social Aspects of Fertility.* Vikash Publishing House Pvt. Ltd., New Delhi.

Chen, L.C., M.C. Gesche, A.I. Chowdhury and W.H. Mosley. 1974. Maternal mortality in rural Bangladesh. *Studies in Family Planning* 5(11): 334-341.

Clark, W.A.K. and P.L. Hosking. 1986. *Statistical Methods for Geographers*. New York: John Wiley and Sons.

Cleland, John. 1990. Maternal education and child survival: Further evidence and explanations. In: John Caldwell, Sally Findely, Pat Caldwell, Gigi Santow, Wendy Cosford, Jennifer Braid, and Daphne Broers-Freeman (eds.), *What we know about health transition: The cultural, social, and behavioural determinants of health*, Vol. 1. Canberra: Australian National University.

Cleland, John; Jane Varrall and Martin Vaessen. 1983. Preference for the sex of children and their influence on reproductive behaviour. World Fertility Survey—Comparative Studies: Cross National Summaries, No. 27. Verbrigrugge International Institute.

Clifford, William B. 1971. Modern and Traditional Value Orientation and Fertility Behaviour: A Socio-Demographic Study. *Demography* 8(1): 37-46.

Das, Madhumita. 2000. Reproductive Health Issues and Health Seeking Behaviour of Women in a Matrilineal Set-up: A Study of Khasi Tribal Women. Ph.D. Thesis, International Institute for Population Sciences, Mumbai-88.

Davis, Kingsley. 1945. *The World Demographic Transition*, Annals of the American Academy of Political and Social Science, Vol. 1.

———1951. *The Population of India and Pakistan*. Princeton University Press, Princeton, NJ.

Davis, K. and Judith Blake. 1956. *Economic Development and Cultural Change*. 4: 211-235.

———. 1983. Demographic Change in Rural South India. *Population Studies* 37(3).

DeGraff, Deborah, Richard E. Bilsborrow, and David K. Guilkey. 1997. Community level determinants of contraceptive use in the Philippines: A structural analysis. *Demography* 34(3): 385-398.

Desai, S. 1994. *Maternal education and child health: Evidence and ideology*. Paper presented at the IUSSP Seminar on Women, Poverty and Demographic Change, Oaxaca, Mexico, October 2-28.

Dharmalingam, A. and S.P. Morgan. 2004. Pervasive Muslim-Hindu Fertility Differences in India. *Demography* 41(3): 529-545.

Dharmalingam, A., K. Navaneetham and S.P. Morgan. 2005. Muslim-Hindu Fertility Differences: Evidence from National Family Health Survey-II. *Economic and Political Weekly* XL (5): 429-436.

Entwisle, Barbara and William M. Mason. 1985. Multilevel effects of socio-economic development and family planning programmes on children ever born. *American Journal of Sociology* 91(3): 616-649.

Entwisle, Barbara, John B. Casterline and A.A. Sayeed. 1989. Villages as contexts for contraceptive behaviour in rural Egypt. *American Sociological Review* 54(6): 1019-1034.

Estrin, Deon J. 1999. Reproductive behaviour is linked to work autonomy, not to employment itself. *International Family Planning Perspectives* 25(1): 50-51.

Freedman, R., A.I. Hermalin and M.C. Chang. 1975. Do statements about desired family size predict fertility? The case of Taiwan. *Demography*: 12(3).

Freedman, Lynn. 1999. Reflections on emerging frameworks of health and human rights. In Jonathan M. Mann, Sofia Gruskin, Michael Gordin and George Annas (eds.), *Health and Human Rights* (Routledge, New York), pp. 227-252.

GoI. 1997. Report of the Sub-Committee on Reproductive Health Research Needs Assessment, National Committee on Research in Human Reproduction, Ministry of Health and Family Welfare, New Delhi.

Goldscheider, Calvin. 1971. *Population, Modernization and Social Structure*. Little, Brown and Company, Boston.

Goldscheider, Calvin and Peter R. Uhlenberg.1969. Minority Group Status and Fertility. *The American Journal of Sociology* 74(4): 361-373.

Goodburn, E., G.J. Ebrahim, and Sishir Senapati. 1990. Strategies educated mother use to ensure the health of their children. *Journal of Tropical Pediatrics* 36: 235-39.

Goodburn, Elizabeth, Rukhsana Gazi, and Mushtaque Chowdhury. 1995. Beliefs and practices regarding delivery and postpartum maternal morbidity in rural Bangladesh. *Studies in Family Planning* 26(1): 22-32.

Govindasamy, P. and B.M. Ramesh. 1997. Maternal Education and the Utilization of Maternal and Child Health Services in India. National Family Health Survey Subject Reports Number 5, IIPS, Mumbai and Macro International Inc., U.S.A.

Greenwell, K. Fern. 1996. Contraceptive method mix menu: Providing healthy choices for women. *World Health Statistics Quarterly* 49(2): 88-93.

Griffiths, Paula and Rob Stephenson. 2001. Understanding users' perspectives of barriers to maternal health care use in Maharashtra, India. *Journal of Biosocial Science* 33(3): 339-359.

Hobcraft, J. 1993. Women's education, child welfare, and child survival: A review of the evidence. *Health Transition Review* 3: 159-75.

Hussain, Majid. 1994. *Encyclopaedia of India*, Vol.-XXIII, Assam, Rima Publishing House, New Delhi.

IIPS, 1995. *National Family Health Survey (MCH and Family Planning), 1992-93: India.* Mumbai: International Institute for Population Sciences.

IIPS and ORC Macro. 2000. *National Family Health Survey (NFHS-2), 1998-99: India.* Mumbai: International Institute for Population Sciences.

Jaffe, A.J. and K. Azumi. 1960. The Birth Rate and Cottage Industries in Under Developed Areas. *Economic Development and Cultural Change* 9(1): 52-63.

Jain, S.P., 1975. *A Study of Population Research in India*: Vol. II, Tata McGraw Hill, New Delhi.

Jain, R.K. 1994. *Dynamics of Reproductive Health Care.* Family Planning Association of India. Panchkula Haryana Branch: 13-16.

James, K.S. and S.B. Nair. 2005. Accelerated Decline in Fertility in India since the 1980s: Trends among Hindu and Muslims. *Economic and Political Weekly*. XL (5): 375-383.

Jeffrey, Roger and Patricia Jeffrey. 1997. *Population Gender and Politics: Demographic Change in Rural North India*, Cambridge University Press, U.K.

Jeffrey, Roger and Patricia Jeffrey. 2000. Religion and Fertility in India. *Economic and Political Weekly* 35: 3252-59.

———2002. A Population Out of Control? Myths About Muslim Fertility in Contemporary India. *World Development* 30(10): 1805-22.

———2005. Saffron Demography, Common Wisdom, Aspirations and Uneven Governmentalities. *Economic and Political Weekly* XL (5): 447-53.

Jones, Gavin and Dorothy Nortman.1968. Roman Catholic Fertility and Family Planning: A Comparative Review of the Research Literature. *Studies in Family Planning* 34: 1-27.

Kapadia, S. 1999. *Women's Reproductive Health: Understanding the Socio-Cultural Context.* Paper presented in the Workshop on Status of Reproductive Health of Women in Gujarat, January 8-9, Baroda.

Kavitha; N. and N. Audinarayana. 1997. Utilisation and determinants of selected MCH care services in rural areas of Tamil Nadu. *Health and Population—Perspectives and Issues* 20(3): 112-125.

Khan, M.E. 1979. *Family Planning Among Muslims in India: A Study of the Reproductive Behaviour of Muslims in an Urban Setting*, Manohar Publications, New Delhi.

———1990. Breastfeeding and Weaning Practices in India. *Asia Pacific Population Journal* 5(1): 71-88.

Kirk, D. 1967. Factor Affecting Muslim Natality. In: O. Schieffelin (eds.), *Muslims Attitude Towards Family Planning*, Population Council, New York.

———1968, Factor Affecting Moslem Fertility. In: Charles B. Nam (eds.), *Population and Society*, pp. 230-242, Houghton Mifflin Company, Boston.

Koenig, M.A., V. Fauveau, A.I. Chowdhury and M.A. Khan. 1988. Maternal mortality in rural Bangladesh: 1976-85. *Studies in Family Planning* 19(2).

Krishnaji, N. and K.S. James. 2005. Religion and Fertility—A Comment. *Economic and Political Weekly* XL (5): 455-58.

Krishnamoorthy, S. 1970. Amenorrhoea in relation to Age, Parity and Breastfeeding. *Bulletin of GIRH & FP* 5(11): 1-13.

Krishnamoorthy, S. and J. Sheela. 2004. Socio-Economic Determinants of Breastfeeding in India. *Demography India* 33(2): 173-192.

Kulkarni, P.M. 1996. *Differentials in the Population Growth of Hindus and Muslims in India, 1981-91*, Monograph Series, No.-1, Population Foundation of India, New Delhi.

Kulkarni, P.M. and M. Alagarajan. 2005. Population Growth, Fertility and Religion in India. *Economic and Political Weekly* XL (5): 403-410.

Kumar, Sanjay. 1997. Women's Work Status and Fertility: Macro and Micro Level Analysis in India and in Selected States. *Demography India* 26(1).

Kumar, Rachel. 2002. Gender in Reproductive and Child Health Policy. *The Economic and Political Weekly* XXXVII (32): 3369-3377.

Ladusingh, L. and Oinam Bijoy. 2004. Loneliness—A Psychological Illness. *Ageing and Society—The Indian Journal of Gerontology* XIV (I & II): 13-22.

Lane, Sundra D. 1994. From population control to reproductive health: an emerging policy agenda. *Social Science and Medicine* 39 (9): 1303-1314.

Lorimer, F., 1954. *Culture and Human Fertility, A Study of the Relation of Cultural Condition to Fertility in non-Industrial and Transitional Societies*, UNESCO, Paris.

Ludden, David. 1996. Introduction, Ayodhya: A Window on the World. In: David Ludden (ed.), *Making India Hindu: Religion, Community and the Politics of Democracy in India*, Oxford University Press, Delhi.

MacDonald, Paul C. and Jack A. Pritchard. 1980. *Williams Obstetrics*. 16th Edition. New York: Appleton-Century-Crofts.

Magadi, Monica K., Nyovani J. Madise, and Robert N. Rodrigues. 2000. Frequency and timing of antenatal care in Kenya: Explaining the variations between women of different communities. *Social Science and Medicine* 51(4): 551-561.

Mahadevan, K. and M. Sumangalam. 1987. *Social Development, Cultural Change and Fertility Decline: A Study of Fertility Change in Kerala*. Sage Publications, New Delhi.

Manda, Samuel Osmand Makandi. 1998: Unobserved family and community effects on infant mortality in Malawi. *Genus* 47: 1841-1854.

Manna, Mausami. 1998. Factors Affecting Fertility Decline and Fertility Variation in 1990s: An Inter-State Analysis. *Economic and Political Weekly* XXXIII (51): 3280-3284.

Mason, K.O. 1992. Family Change and Support of Elderly in Asia: What Does We Know? *Asia Pacific Population Journal* 7(3): East West Centre Reprint Series No. 286.

McDaniel, Susan A. 1996. Towards a synthesis of feminist and demographic perspectives on fertility. *The Sociological Quarterly* 37 (1): 83-104.

———2000. *The demographic category as leaky gender boundary*, paper presented at the American Sociological Association meeting, Washington, August 12-16, 2000.

Miles-Doan, Rebecca and Karia L. Brewster. 1998. The impact of type of employment on women's use of pre-natal-care services and family planning in urban Cebu, the Phillipines. *Studies in Family Planning* 29(1): 69-78.

Motashaw, Nergesh D. 1997. Root causes of maternal mortality: Infancy to motherhood. *The Journal of Family Welfare* 43 (2): 4-14.

Moulasha, K. 2000. Religious Affiliation and Fertility Behaviour in Maharashtra State: A Study of Hindus and Muslims, Ph.D. Thesis, International Institute for Population Sciences, Mumbai-88.

Nath, D.C. and A.K. Deka. 2004. The Importance of Son in a Traditional Society. *Demography India* 33(1): 33-46.

Nath, D.C. and K.C. Land. 1994. Sex Preference and Third Birth Intervals in a Traditional Indian Society. *Journal of Biosocial Science* 26: 95-106.

Nath, D.C. and G. Goswami. 1997. Determination of Breastfeeding Patterns in an Urban Society of India. *Human Biology* 69(4): 557-573.

Nath, D.C. and L.D. Leonetti. 2001. Correlates of Coital Patterns in a Traditional Indian Society. In: R.C. Yadava *et al.* (eds.), *Dynamics of Population Change (Emerging issues of 21st Century)*. Shipra Publication, Delhi, pp. 57-67.

Nwakoby, Boniface N. 1994. Use of obstetric services in rural Nigeria. *Journal of the Royal Society of Health* 114(3): 132-136.

NFHS-I, Assam, 1992-93. Population Research Centre, Gauhati University and International Institute for Population Sciences, Mumbai-88.

NFHS-II, Assam, 1998-99. ORC Macro and International Institute for Population Sciences, Mumbai-88.

Nuwaha, F. and B. Amooti-Kaguna. 1999. Predictors of home deliveries in Rakai District, Uganda. *African Journal of Reproductive Health* 3(2): 79-86.

Obermeyer, Carla Makhlouf. 1993. Culture, maternal health care, and women's status: A comparison of Morocco and Tunisia. *Studies in Family Planning* 24(6): 354-365.

Omran, A.R. 1992. *Family Planning in the legacy of Islam*. London: Routlege.

Pachauri, Saroj. 1994. Women's Reproductive Health in India: Research Needs and Priorities. In: J. Gittlesohn, M.E. Bentley PI Pelto, M. Nag, S. Pachauri, A.D. Harrison, L.T. Landman (eds.), *Listening to Women Talk about Their Health Issues and Evidence from India*. The Ford Foundation and Har-Anand Publications, New Delhi.

Padmini, I.K. and S. Krishnamoorthy. 1988. Differences in Breastfeeding Practices between Family Types in a Tamil Nadu Village. *Journal of Family Welfare* 35(1): 61-64.

Pandey, A., B.N. Bhattacharya, D. Sahu and R. Sultana. 2004. Are Too Early, Too Quickly and Too Many Births the High Risk? An Analysis of Infant Mortality in India Using National Family Health Survey. *Demography India* 33(2): 127-157.

Pandey, Arvind, Minja K. Choe, Norman Y. Luther, Damodar Sahu and Jagdish Chand. 1998. *Infant and Child Mortality in India.* National Family Health Survey Subject Reports No. 11. International Institute for Population Sciences, Mumbai and East-West Centre Programme on Population, Honolulu, Hawaii, USA.

Park, J.E. and K. Park. 1989. *Textbook of Preventive and Social Medicine.* 12th Edition. Jabalpur: M/s Banarsidas Bhanot Publishers.

Pebley, Anne R., Noreen Goldman, and German Rodriguez. 1996. Prenatal and delivery care and childhood immunization in Guatemala: Do family and community matter? *Demography* 33(2): 231-247.

Perkin, G.W. 1968. Assessment of reproductive risk in non-pregnant women. *American Journal of Obstetrics and Gynaecology* 101(5): 709-711.

Qadeer, Imrana. 1998. Reproductive Health: A Public Health Perspective. *Economic and Political Weekly* XXXIII (41): 2675-2685.

Rahman, M. 1996. *Child Mortality and Fertility Regulation Behaviour in Bangladesh: Implications for Family Planning Programme.* ICDDR. B. Centre for Health and Population Research MCH—FP Extension Project (Rural), Working Paper No. 115.

Rahman, M. and Julie Da Vanzo. 1993. Gender Preference and Birth Spacing in Matlab, Bangladesh. *Demography* 30(3).

Rajan, S.I. 2005. District Level Fertility Estimates for Hindus and Muslims. *Economic and Political Weekly* XL (5): 437-446.

Raj Hans. 1996. *Population Studies.* Surjeet Publications, Delhi.

Rajendran, T. 1997. Socio-economic differentials in fertility and family size of sterilisation acceptors of the 1980s in rural Karnataka. *The Journal of Family Welfare* 43(4): 46-58.

Rajput, K.S. 2001. The Religious Composition of Population of Assam: The Changing Trend. Term paper presented as a partial requirement for the fulfilment of degree of Master of Population Studies, IIPS, Mumbai-88.

———2002. Safe Motherhood: A Human Right Issue. In: Aparna Mahanta (ed.), *Human Rights and Women of North East India*, Centre for Women's Studies, Dibrugarh University. Assam.

Ram, R.B. and R.B. Mehta.1983. Some Aspects of Fertility in a Rural Sector of Bihar, Monograph Series No. 73, PRC, Patna University.

Reddy, J.P. 1986. *Changing Patterns of Nuptiality and Natality in Urban Muslim.* Paper presented in the National Seminar on Changing Family and Marriage Patterns in Different Social Systems, Tamil University, Thanjavur.

Rinchart, W. and A. Kols. 1984. Healthier mothers and children through family planning. *Population Report*, Series 1(27): 663.

Rutenberg, Naomi and Susan Cotts Watkins. 1997. The buzz outside the clinics: Conversations and contraception in Nyanza Province, Kenya. *Studies in Family Planning* 28(4): 290-307.

Retherford, R.D. and M.K. Choe. 1993. *Statistical Models for Causal Analysis*. New York: John Wiley and Sons.

Roy, T.K., J. Gill and V. Sharma. 1997. Regional Variation in Fertility and Utilisation of Family Welfare Services in Uttar Pradesh. In: Kamla Gupta and Arvind Pandey (eds.), *Population and Development in Uttar Pradesh*, B.R. Publishing Corporation, New Delhi.

Sharif, A.S. 1994. *Some Socio-Economic and Demographic Aspects of Population according to Religion in India*. Centre for Study of Society and Secularism, Bombay.

Shariff, Abusalleh. 1995. Socio-Economic and Demographic Differentials between Hindu and Muslims in India. *Economic and Political Weekly* 30 (46): 2947-2952.

Sharma, A.K. and B.D. Mishra. 1978. Fertility differentials in India—An analysis of census fertility data. *The Journal of Family Welfare* 25(2).

Shrivastava, O.S. 1996. *Demography and Population Studies*. Vikash Publishing House Pvt. Ltd., New Delhi.

Smith, D.P. 1980. Age at First Marriage, World Fertility Survey, Comparative Studies, Cross National Summaries, Number 7, International Statistical Institute, 1980.

Srivastava, H.C. *et al.* 1998. *Fertility Transition in India: State Level Analysis based on SRS Data, 1971-1991*, Monograph, International Institute for Population Sciences, Mumbai-88.

Stanfield, J.P. and A. Galazka. 1984. Neonatal Tetanus in the World Today. *Bulletin of the World Health Organization* 62(4).

Stephenson, Rob and Amy Ong Tsui. 2002. Contextual Influences on Reproductive Health Services Use in Uttar Pradesh, India. *Studies in Family Planning* 33 (4): 309-320.

Swenson, I. And P.A. Harpner. 1979. High-risk maternal factors related to fetal wastage in rural Bangladesh. *Journal of Biosocial Science* 11: 465-471.

Terry, G.B. 1975. Rival explanation in the work fertility relationship. *Population Studies* 29(2).

United Nations. 1987. Fertility Behaviour in the context of Development: Evidence from World Fertility Survey. *Population Studies* No. 100 (New York, Department of International Economic and Social Affairs, UN).

———1993. *Women's Education and Fertility Behaviour: A Case Study of Rural Maharashtra, India*, New York: United Nations.

———1994. *Programme of Action of the United Nations Conference on Population Development*, New York: United Nations.

———1995. *Women's Education and Fertility Behaviour: Recent Evidence from the Demographic and Health Surveys*, New York: United Nations.

Visaria, L. 1974. Religious Differentials in Fertility. In: Ashish Bose *et al.* (eds.), *Population in India's Development: 1947-2000*, Vikas Publishing House Pvt. Ltd., New Delhi.

Von Korff, M., T. Koepsell, S. Curry, and P. Dieh. 1992. Multilevel research in epidemiological research on health behaviours and outcomes. *American Journal of Epidemiology* 135: 1077-1082.

Westoff, Charles F. 1959. *Religion and Fertility in Metropolitan America,* In Thirty Years Research in Human Fertility: Retrospect and Prospect: Annual Conference of Milbank Memorial Fund, New York; Milbank Memorial Fund.

WHO. 1993. *Women's Needs and Perspectives in Reproductive Health,* Report of an African Regional Workshop, Nairobi, 24-26 November.

Williamson, Nancy, E. 1976. *Sons or Daughters: A Cross Cultural Survey of Parental Preference.* Beverly Hill, Sage.

World Bank (1993): *Investing in Health.* World Development Report. New York: Oxford University Press.

Index